AF601788

Keto Diet Guide and Balanced Weight Loss

Compare Types of Diet and Pick The Healthiest

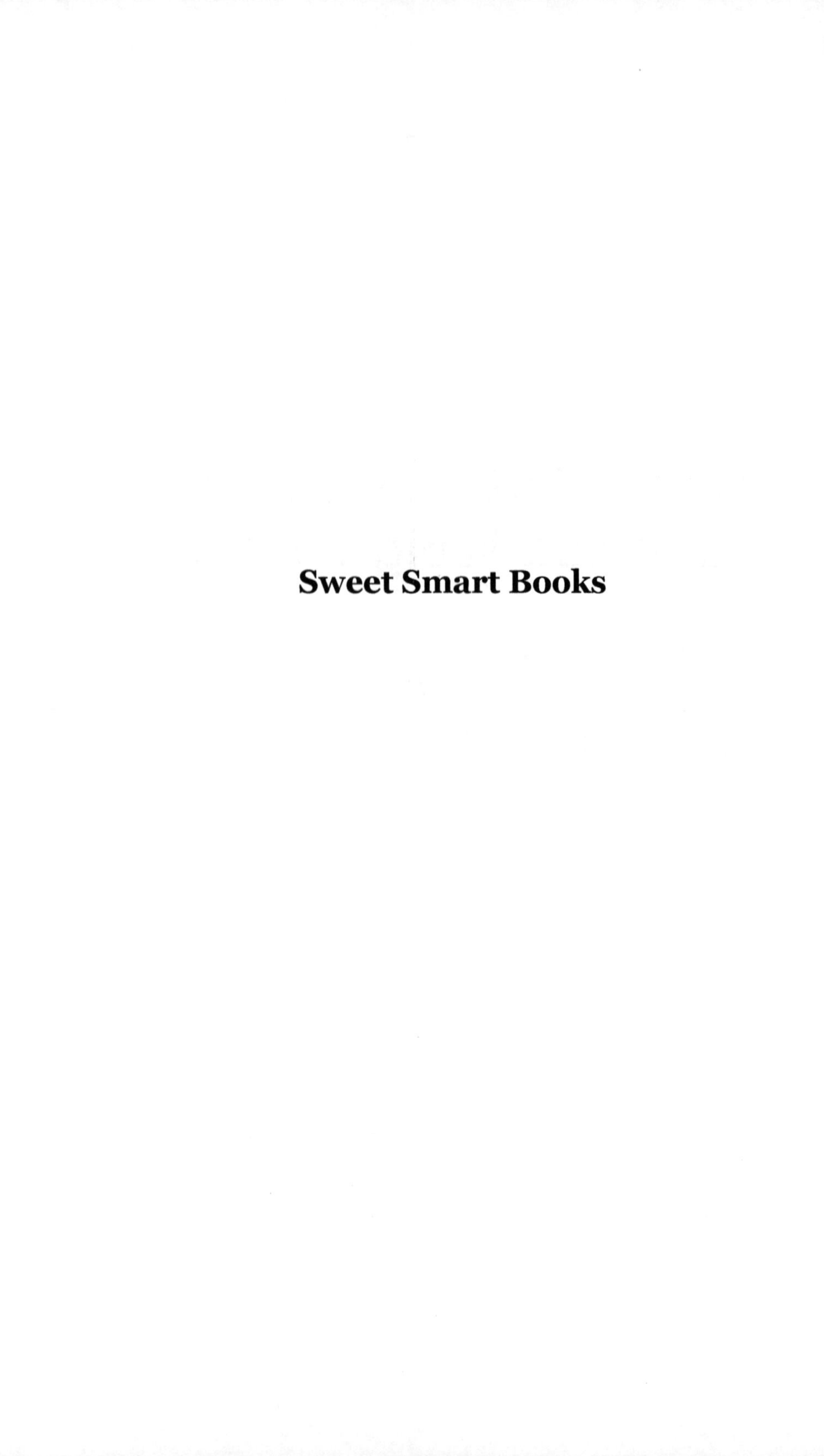

Sweet Smart Books

Table of Contents

Introduction
Chapter 1: Dieting and Goals - Working Together
Benefits of Dieting
How to Create Goals
Combing Effective Goals and Dieting
Making Sure You Get The Nutrition You Need
Chapter 2: Mindset - Tackling the Struggles of Change
Misconceptions About Dieting
Dieting And Mental Barriers
Overcoming Addictions: Sugar and Caffeine
Overcoming The Odds
Chapter 3: Keto Diet—Everything You Need To
Keto Diet—What Sets it Apart?
Studies with Regard To the Keto Diet
Food
Benefits of A Keto Diet
Disadvantages of the Keto Diet
Chapter 4: Keto Diet -Recipes to Try
Recipe 1: Creamy Tuscan Garlic Chicken

Recipe 2: Baked Eggs with Zoodles and Avocado

Recipe 3: Cheesy Cauliflower Breadsticks

Recipe 4: Prosciutto & Cauliflower Bites

Recipe 5: Keto Broccoli Salad

Recipe 6: Keto Meatballs in Sauce

Chapter 5: Diet Types—Paleo, Vegan, Low Carb, and Blood Type Diets

Paleo Diet Explained

Paleo Diet: Benefits and Drawbacks

Paleo Diet: Steps to Take

Vegan Diet Explained

Vegan Diet: Benefits and Drawbacks

Low Carb Diet Explained

Low Carb Diet: Benefits and Drawbacks

Blood Type Diet

Advantages and Disadvantages of Blood Type Diet

Blood Type Diets: Foods For Each Type

Chapter 6: Diet Types: Dukan, Atkins, Intermittent Fasting

Dukan Diet Explained

Dukan Diet: Benefits and Drawbacks

Atkins Diet

Atkins: Benefits and Drawbacks

Intermittent Fasting Explained

Intermittent Fasting Benefits and Drawbacks

Wrapping Up The Diets

Chapter 7: Choosing a Diet For Your Lifestyle

How to Overcome The Mental Battles of Dieting

Finding Your Voice

Taking Down Bad Habits

Adding New Habits

Preventing Self-Sabotage

How To Draw Up A Meal Plan

Conclusion

References

Introduction

If you were to search on Google how to lose weight, you may just find yourself overwhelmed with thousands of articles that often contradict each other left, right, and center. You will also find a vast amount of businesses and organizations advertising that their weight loss classes, products, and shortcuts will leave you with results, guaranteed. Oftentimes, you may even be taken to videos promising to share the most common tricks, only to have a marketeer ramble on upon their life's journey, market their company, brag about their students or members, and finally end it with a 'trick' that you may have already known.

The search for answers is tiring, especially when it comes to dieting. This book is meant to demystify some of the most challenging aspects of your weight loss journey. Combining some of the most popular and effective dieting methods, *Keto Diet Guide and Balanced Weight Loss* focuses on keto dieting and several other effective diets. Keep in mind that different forms of dieting will be effective for different people since everyone's body responds differently to what they eat. Take the time to investigate all the options and choose a plan according to your body type, budget, and lifestyle. Even a person's daily schedule affects what kind of healthy dieting a person should adopt. For example, someone who actively works at a hospital may find intermittent fasting inconvenient at best if not dangerous. Considering there are spotty eating times, there is no solid way to plan different eating and fasting windows around their demanding tasks. However, someone who has taken on a desk job is certainly free to consider it.

This book also dives into the mental battles and bad habits one will have to overcome. For you to fully succeed in dieting and weight loss, no journey of health comes quickly (there is no miraculous quick fix either), but the rewards of the hard work do make this worth your while. The path to healthy living is at your fingertips. All you need to do is read, choose a plan, and stick to it. If you do not reach your goals over a designated time, then you should reconsider changing your diet. All in all, remember to be gracious and patient with yourself. This book focuses on a realistic pathway, and there are bound to be mistakes made now and then since many people are still trying to figure out the building blocks of weight loss.

Weight loss is not easy, but it is not complicated either. It's up to you to shape and fashion the path you intend to take. With the right tools and knowledge, you may even surprise yourself with where you end up. This book will assist you in avoiding common mistakes made by others and adopting practices that will improve your overall health. This book does not offer quick solutions or shortcuts to losing weight in an unhealthy way. It all starts with a simple choice to change little by little until you find yourself at your goal.

Chapter 1: Dieting and Goals - Working Together

A common misconception many people have about dieting and exercising is that you can outrun any unhealthy meal. Doing a push-up won't necessarily fix the two to three chocolate bars you ate earlier. And despite all the hilarious memes of people eating junk food while exercising, it is sad to say that exercising won't simply melt away the food you consume.

Your diet and your lifestyle have the highest effect on your weight loss journey. It is for this reason that your diet plan and goals need to go hand in hand in order for you to see true accomplishment.

Benefits of Dieting

Generally, it is well known that the benefits of dieting extend well beyond losing weight. You should consider healthy eating to boost your overall health and reduce the risk of medical issues. Here is an in-depth look at some of the benefits.

One benefit healthy dieting has is giving your immune system a boost. Nobody likes getting sick, and doctor visits are expensive!

A healthy diet helps keep you from getting sick, but it also helps you maintain a healthy weight. There will come a point where you have reached your weight loss goal. However, returning back to old bad habits will simply wash all your hard work away. Therefore, focusing on maintaining a healthy diet is a surefire way to help you maintain your ideal weight forever without too much of a struggle.

You may find an increased boost in energy when focusing on a healthy diet. With a better flow of energy, your body rewards you with healthy hair, nails, and even skin! Getting the proper nutrition will allow your body to work at an optimal level. Once you have a healthy diet, you will see the differences not only in your weight but in your general appearance as well.

Going a little deeper, your heart, one of the most important muscles in your body, is certainly affected by the food you eat. According to The American Heart Association (AHA), almost half of adults in the United States live with some form of cardiovascular disease (Crichton-Stuart, 2020). This means that over a million people have heart problems, and the primary cause is an unhealthy diet. A poor diet can contribute to high blood pressure, a concern due to it causing an increased risk of heart attacks, strokes, and even heart failure. Studies have shown that approximately 80%

of these conditions are preventable (Crichton-Stuart, 2020).

These health risks can especially be prevented through the embracing of a healthy diet and lifestyle. It is said you are what you eat, and this is certainly true. Eating healthy foods that reduce blood pressure as well as reducing bad cholesterol are benefits that come with a good diet. This generally means a person should eat complete servings of fruits and vegetables, as well as avoiding the amount of sugar they consume. Avoiding the excessive sodium contained in fast foods and cutting out regular table salts where needed is also a good method of decreasing your blood pressure.

Having a healthy diet has also been shown to significantly reduce the risk of cancer, where the increased antioxidants from healthy meals help to lower the likelihood of you getting a disease. Generally, foods with high antioxidants are leafy greens, pumpkins, carrots, and even nuts and seeds. Being obese, unfortunately, also increases your risk of cancer and other diseases. Taking on a healthy diet will change your life.

Having a healthy diet will boost your mood. This will have a positive effect on your overall living situation, as well as your responses to stress. Your diet and your mood are closely linked together, and those with unhealthy eating habits also tend to have it worse (especially if binge and emotional eating occur regularly).

You may be surprised to learn that eating healthy meals will improve your overall memory. It certainly boosts your cognition and brain health, as well as reducing the chances of you suffering from dementia or cognitive decline.

For someone who suffers from diabetes, a healthy meal is a sure way to help you boost your health and reduce the risks associated with diabetes. With good nutrition, you can maintain control over your level of glucose, maintain a good weight, and manage your cholesterol.

Your bones and your teeth will also get stronger. Parents and grandparents weren't lying when they said candy and sugar damage your teeth. Good foods rich in calcium such as dairy, cauliflower, and broccoli can boost the strength of your bones and teeth.

You may find yourself sleeping better as well when you start eating healthy and reducing alcohol intake (which both contribute to sleep apnoea).

Your improved diet may give your children a better chance of a healthy lifestyle because children learn by example. In the long term, if they were to learn how to cook healthy meals, they are more likely to take those lessons with them wherever they go. You could also be a very positive influence on your peers and their extended family.

All in all, living a healthy lifestyle will bring multiple benefits into your life. It is uncertain to know exactly which ones will come on stronger than others, considering that every person's body is different. It may take you longer to lose weight than other people, or you may lose weight faster than others. It depends upon your metabolic rate and age, among other factors. As a disclaimer please consult a doctor before making a dietary change. Keep all of these things in mind and have realistic expectations when it comes to adopting a healthy lifestyle. Let it come to you. Enjoy every benefit that you do come across. Remember, there is no magic formula or hard set of rules when it comes to dieting. What benefits you see will depend on

How to Create Goals

Setting up no plan is planning to fail. You need to plan your meals according to your new healthy lifestyle, rather than going day by day in hopes that you eat healthily. Everyone knows that any battle strategy without a well-thought-out plan is destined to fail. Dieting is certainly no war in a physical aspect. However, you are battling some mental and social pressures that come up in your everyday life. It is not easy to adapt and change your lifestyle because you have years of bad habits to unlearn. Therefore, it is good to set yourself up for success by formulating a good and sound plan. As much as you can create a thorough and effective plan, you also need to learn to follow it.

First, let's start with breaking the tradition of when to create a plan. The answer to that is any time and at any place. Whether it's right now, in the middle of the day, or the new year, you can change your life within a split second. If you wait until the new year and you hit some roadblocks along the way, you will just keep putting off the commitment until the next year. How on earth are you supposed to keep up? People forget that on New Year's Eve, there are many celebrations like parties and family gatherings. If you want to set up goals for weight loss, this does make it far more difficult than if you were to plan it later on in the year. You can start your plan anytime, any day. This is a good mindset to adopt. There is no perfect time to start a new goal, there's only a good plan.

Secondly, you want to focus on SMART goals. SMART is an acronym that stands for:

- Specific
- Measurable
- Achievable
- Realistic
- Timely.

It means that there is a specific way for you to form and plan achievable goals.

Now, take a look at the first letter in the acronym: Specific. This means that the goal is well-defined and detailed. It is easy to say, "I'll be eating healthy from now on" without knowing how or where, or when. Which foods are you going to eat? What can you truly afford? How long will you maintain this lifestyle? Will it have a good impact on your weight? Claiming just to eat healthily is very much like wandering in the woods with the map from a book belonging in the fiction store. You will certainly have an idea of what the place looks like, but without proper guiding trails, you will find yourself hopelessly lost.

The second letter is measurable. This means your goal has to fit within a specific time frame to measure the progress that you are making in your day-to-day life. If you cannot measure something, how do you expect to achieve it? It is best to plan a weekly diet to lose a certain amount, instead of saying you want to reach your weight goal in no specified amount of time. Not only is this unmotivating, but it could also work to discourage anyone who wants to walk a path of weight loss. If something takes a long time to achieve, it all comes down to the little accomplishments along the way.

SMART goals are achievable. This may sound obvious, but people often place unrealistic expectations upon themselves, especially when it comes to weight loss. Many people want a quick fix scheme that will have them at their ideal weight within a week. In the end, a person can only lose so much realistically in a healthy way. Making your goal achievable is setting yourself up for success.

Now, let's explore the second to last letter: realistic. A realistic goal has to be practical, while also considering your lifestyle. Stress factors and other reasons make otherwise achievable goals difficult to accomplish. You have to personalize your goals according to your routine and your life. If you stick to a plan that does not consider anything about your life, even if the goal is achievable for some people, it certainly won't be for you.

Lastly is the word timely. Setting time frames and due dates for your goals is one of the most important aspects of keeping them. It's one thing to say that you will achieve a goal, but it is another to set a time for it. People slack when they think they have time. When they are running out of time, action tends to be taken.

Combing Effective Goals and Dieting

It is best to create effective and smart goals that work hand in hand with a strategic dieting plan. Whether it is keto, intermittent fasting, or other methods you may come across.

This is normally termed a meal plan, where you plan your meals according to a specific format. There is no perfect meal plan, just like there is no perfect weight loss program. All one can do is try, test, and adapt them according to your lifestyle.

First things first, you need to make sure you are 100% ready. When deciding on a diet, there is certainly no time for turning back. Your goals need to be aligned, and you need to set the course. Expect a few setbacks and struggles (see chapter two), and create a plan. If you do not create a plan, you are planning to fail.

So how do you create a meal plan? Firstly, set aside a certain amount of time for yourself in your house and review your schedule. It is best to figure out yourself when the best times are for you to cook. When taking on a diet, this will become essential as fast foods and restaurants will hinder your weight loss journey. But, do not avoid the occasional restaurant outing and social gathering, either. The plan is for you to lose weight, not become a hermit.

When possible, cut out all processed foods, and take extra time to cook. It doesn't matter if you can't cook every day. Just plan ahead! If you are more available on Mondays, Thursdays, and Saturdays, then cook extra meals for Tuesdays, Wednesdays, Fridays, and Sundays. A fridge and freezer will certainly spare you from spoiling any food, as well as snatching away your excuses for fast food. Keep your pantry well-stocked with healthy foods that you prepared!

Next, it is time to choose your recipes following the diet you want to undertake. Make sure the meal prep times fit in with your schedule so you aren't stuck cooking during all of your free time. You are guaranteed to order fast food if you plan a two-hour recipe when you only have forty minutes to prepare it. Logical planning will get you a long way in your journey. Take into consideration what you also have in your pantry. If you need to buy all the ingredients, then maybe you should reconsider your recipe rather than your budget. Find out recipes where you regularly have a good number of items. If you can afford to purchase all new ingredients, then go for it! People will be in awe of your new healthy lifestyle.

Now that you have decided on your recipes and your schedule, it is time to plan your recipes within the time slots you have allocated to cook. This may take some time and experimentation, as one is not likely to get it perfect the first time. Be flexible with the recipes and allow room for change if absolutely need be. Remember, there is no singular right answer when it comes to weight loss and dieting. For the sake of actually losing it, one has to bend the rules now and then. Remember to add a cheat day every week. This doesn't mean to eat in excess and throw six days of hard work down the drain. It simply means allowing room for other meals such as fast foods that you wouldn't normally allow for any other day in the week.

The next step is to form and shape a grocery list when you have the times, recipes, and ingredients gathered together. Make sure you know how all your foods are stocked as well to make sure you don't make a double purchase. This can cause food to go to waste and stretch your wallet unnecessarily. Depending on what suits you and your habits, consider buying either once a week or once a month. Do not consider going in every day, as you would be exposing yourself to far more temptation. Also, a good rule to remember while shopping is never to visit a shop on an empty stomach. Otherwise, it may result in overspending, especially on the junk foods that defeat the entire purpose of your weight loss and diet.

Time to go shopping! After eating your snack and having your plans together, you are finally ready. You can consider using digital tools to keep track of your items or stick to the traditional paper and pen. Consider grocery shopping online through safe and secure platforms if you find your schedule to be too busy, or the shops to be too full of temptation. The modern world gives you many tools to use for your health. You can also cut out a lot of time that you may need in your schedule. The availability of online shopping also eliminates the excuse that you don't have time to shop. If you have your shopping list at hand, all that is truly left is a few taps of the button and you have your groceries. Some may require you to simply drive and pick up. Not much different from a fast food restaurant is it?

After you're done shopping, it is time to cook! Try your best to stick as closely to your meal plan as possible. The first few weeks may be tough, but soon you will find yourself getting used to it. That is a great sign, as it means you have overcome many of the mental hurdles that tend to surround people that decide to make meal changes.

So, you have set your SMART weight loss goals and you have laid down your meal plan. The question is what next? All the physical aspects are completed, but you are still faced with the reality of your greatest enemy: yourself. When it comes to weight loss, there is generally an immense mental battle a person has to overcome. But do not fear, you are not alone in this war, and many can help you along the way.

Making Sure You Get The Nutrition You Need

When starting with a new diet, a person often clambers in with no idea on whether or not they should tweak and change certain aspects for their health. They may often not even be aware of the nutrition your body needs even when taking on a diet. The reason why this is so crucial is to avoid getting any deficiencies and health problems when a diet may be lacking a certain nutrient and needs a supplement. For example, going vegan does make you lack vitamin B-12. If supplements are not taken, then a vegan can have some serious and permanent nerve damage. Therefore, it is best to take your nutrition seriously when applying a diet to your life.

In summary, there are six essential nutrients your body needs. They are known as vitamins, proteins, minerals, fats, water, and carbohydrates.

Vitamins are first in line, they are forms of micronutrients that have multiple health benefits. This does have an impact on your bone, teeth, skin, and metabolism. Some vitamins go as far as boosting your immune system, helping out with the brain and nervous system, and keeping your circulatory system healthy. Thirteen vitamins have been divided into two groups. One is fat-soluble, meaning it can be stored. Others are water-soluble, which means they cannot be stored and have to be consumed every single day.

The fat-soluble vitamins are Vitamin D, A, E and K. Water Soluble vitamins are all the B vitamins and vitamin C, thiamine (B-1), cyanocobalamin (B-12), B-6, riboflavin (B-2), pantothenic acid (B-5), niacin (b-3), folate and folic acid (B-9) and biotin (B-7).

Most people who have a rich diet in fruits, vegetables, and lean proteins are not likely to suffer from deficiencies. However, whenever you cut out a food group that may have digestive conditions, you should consider taking supplements to avoid or reduce any forms of deficiencies that may take place.

The next nutrition minerals are the second form of micronutrients the body needs. They are also divided up into two specific groups. These are known as major and trace minerals. You need a healthy balance of each for your body to truly function at its best.

The major minerals are magnesium, calcium, sulfur, phosphorus, potassium, chloride, and sodium. They play a role in healthier skin, hair, and nails, the health and strength of your bones, and the levels of water in your body.

The trace minerals are iron, selenium, iodine, zinc, manganese, chromium, copper, molybdenum, and fluoride. They are important for blood clotting, bone strengthening, carrying oxygen, strengthening the immune system, and keeping blood pressure healthy.

A person who eats a lot of red meats, iodized table salt, seafood, vegetables, fruits, eggs, whole grains, beans and legumes, poultry, fortified bread and cereals, milk and other dairy products, and nuts and seeds tend to consume enough minerals.

You are probably no stranger to protein, but did you know that it is a macronutrient necessary to help out your antibodies and hormones? It also plays a role in the growth of your hair, skin, bones, and muscles as well as serving as a fuel source for tissues and cells. A person can often get protein through poultry, red meats, legumes and beans, eggs, nuts, soy, certain grains, fish and seafood, and dairy products. It is best to make sure that you consume enough protein for your body, especially if you are exercising. Furthermore, ensuring that you have enough protein can also prevent extreme hunger cravings, specifically for those who are on an intermittent fasting diet.

Fats are often stigmatized and associated with bad health, yet a person does need a certain kind of fat to stay healthy. Fat helps with your energy levels and plays certain roles in boosting a range of your functions. It is important to focus on eating monounsaturated and polyunsaturated fats while avoiding trans and saturated fats.

Fats play a role in blood clotting, the building of cells as well as cell growth and ironically enough reducing the risks of heart disease as well as type 2 diabetes. It also has a part in one's immune system, hormone production, and blood sugar as well as the absorption of one's vitamins and minerals. You can normally find healthy fats in foods such as fish, nuts, coconut oils, vegetable oils, and seeds.

Carbs are also quite essential for the body. They tend to provide energy for the cells and tissues. There are two forms of carbs known as simple and complex. It is highly recommended for everyone to limit their simple carbs and eat mostly complex carbs. This is because complex carbs tend to digest more slowly, resulting in less of a blood sugar spike in comparison to simple carbs. Complex carbs help with brain function, your nervous system, digestion, immune system health, and energy levels.

Complex carbs tend to be quinoa, vegetables, fruits, whole-grain pieces of bread, pasta, and other baked goods, oatmeal and barley, and brown rice.

Water—without it you just wouldn't survive. Water is likely to be the most important nutrient out of all of them, as a person can potentially survive a few weeks without food but only a few days without water. Even mild forms of dehydration often tend to cause headaches as it impairs cognitive and physical functioning.

It all makes sense when you realize that people are mostly made up of water, and every cell needs water to work. Water plays a role in flushing out toxins, absorbing shock, lubrication, hydration, nutrient transportation, and far more.

It is best to drink natural water that hasn't been sweetened. If you do not like the taste, then consider flavoring it with some drops of lemon or other citrus fruits. You also tend to get in the water by eating fruits, such as watermelon. Do not focus on getting your water sources from any sugary drinks or caffeine.

Now that you know the six essential nutrients it is best to consider this when taking on a diet. Any diet that cuts out food groups needs to have some form of supplement to make sure that you lose weight, function optimally, and never suffer from any form of deficiency. You will also be far wiser in this approach than many others who decide to walk into a diet blindly without making any necessary adaptations. No diet form is perfect, and to keep yourself healthy in your weight loss journey, you need to make sure you still get everything your body needs to function at its utmost best. So do yourself a massive favor, and make sure you get all the necessary nutrients during this weight loss journey.

Chapter 2: Mindset - Tackling the Struggles of Change

Imagine Jack wants to lose weight. He set up a good plan and a reward system. He then decides to pump iron in the gym and eat a good healthy diet. One day, however, he stubbed his toe and cracked his window. He is in a foul mood and decided to skip his workout. No problem, as long as he eats correctly, no damage would really be done. Except, being an emotional eater, he caves into temptation and gulps down a huge plate of a burger and fries. This brings his mood even further down as not only has he cheated on his meal, but he also skipped his workout. His mind spirals down a drain of self-doubt and he simply gives up.

There is no doubt that the biggest problem when it comes to dieting is the mental battles. A mindset change is desperately needed when changing your lifestyle. There's something about food that just makes things infinitely harder than any other habits. It may be easier to get up 15 minutes earlier than to swap out a doughnut for fruit. It is certainly easier to add more work on your computer than to stand up and do a few exercises. It is not completely clear why a person struggles so much with dieting and exercise. All that is known is that it is a mental struggle and once you overcome the mental struggle you are bound to succeed.

Misconceptions About Dieting

The first mental battle is a mindset change for dieting. There are many misconceptions that run across the internet as well as other people's ideas. With so many myths and misinformation, it is no wonder how often people fail to meet their goals. This is quite sad, but a harsh truth. Many times when the truth is distorted, the effectiveness of any practice, especially a diet, is taken away.

The first myth is that a person needs to cut carbs out of their diet. Yes, there are certainly different kinds of carbs a person should actually avoid. These are called simple carbs. Complex carbs are actually very important for people. They carry nutrients and energy in order throughout the body.

Secondly, there is the idea that skipping breakfast can help you lose weight. Eating a healthy breakfast helps you control your hunger throughout the day. It can also help you to say no to any junk food and unhealthy snacks that happen to come your way. But, there is no scientific study or reports that result in direct weight gain when someone skips their morning breakfast. If you are not hungry first thing in the morning, then you should consider listening to your body. When you are hungry and ready to eat, consider helping yourself with healthy foods.

Just like skipping breakfast in the morning, there is the misconception that eating at night will also cause weight gain. Generally, people who do eat late at night can put on extra weight. The reasoning behind this is not the time that people eat, but what they decide to eat. Normally, people who eat midnight snacks choose high-calorie foods. Therefore, it is not the fact that you eat at night that causes you to gain weight, but rather the quality of the food that you decide to eat. This makes all the difference in the world.

Another idea is that fasting will help you lose weight very quickly. However, there's a fine line between fasting and starvation. Most of the time, fasting methods are practiced incorrectly and dangerously. It is best to educate yourself on intermittent fasting and other fasting methods, focusing on what to eat before you fast and what to eat after your fast. Cutting out your meals without any preparation and knowledge could cause you to lose muscle rather than fat, due to placing yourself in too deep of a starvation mode.

There is another bad mindset when it comes to dieting. This is the idea that you have to lose weight slowly in order to be able to keep the weight off. While it is generally true that some people have gained back all the weight that they have lost, it does not mean it will happen to everyone. People who are overweight are more successful in losing their weight at a faster rate, and it is very likely that they will not be getting it back. The biggest problem arises when people do not practice the correct eating methods. Many people lose weight by slowing down their metabolism. But the moment they add the correct amount of calories again, even if they are eating healthy, they will gain weight. This is all because of incorrect eating. So, it is recommended to lose weight slowly. Not because of your metabolism, but to help give you time to turn your bad eating habits into good ones.

There is also a common myth that once you start losing weight, you'll keep losing weight. This, however, all depends upon your metabolic rate. Your metabolic rate is how many calories your body burns when it's resting. It changes as your weight goes down. It also depends upon a variety of factors. These are things like your height, your gender at birth, and your current age. Other items can have an influence, such as your muscle mass. You will certainly lose more weight if you have more muscle in your body. This is because your muscles burn more calories while your body is resting.

Another lie that is unfortunately spread throughout the web and by health companies is the idea that supplements can help you lose weight. There's actually nothing that is on the market that can increase your metabolism. Certainly, supplements can assist in decreasing your appetite, but it doesn't change your metabolism. There are certain supplements that are even considered fat burners that contain herbs and chemicals like caffeine. These can actually be very dangerous.

Some push the falsehood that obesity is not even genetic. However, some people, unfortunately, do have genetic factors that lead to obesity. The good news about this is that you can remedy this. If you're more conscious about your diet and the level of activity, you can certainly turn the tables in your favor.

There is another idea out there that you can be healthy and overweight. This isn't completely true. Being overweight can bring a variety of health risks and issues. There is also the opposite misconception that thin people are healthier. That is also not generally the case. Using the body mass index (BMI) calculator is not always an accurate way to gauge healthy weight, considering that it does not accurately measure your health. It does not take into account your visceral fat (the fat that surrounds the organs in your body). People who use BMI can have false ideas about their weight. A person who is an athlete can still be recorded as obese even though they're fit. This is all due to the miscalculations in the BMI. There is certainly no perfect singular form when calculating your health.

Another misconception is that what you eat doesn't matter if you exercise more. There is a saying that goes, "you cannot outrun a bad diet." Unfortunately, this is true. You can certainly burn 500 calories by running five miles or doing one extremely long hour of high-intensity exercise. But it is easier to attain a 500 calorie deficit by simply reducing the amount you eat. You will certainly have a hard time losing weight when you eat badly and over-exercise to make up for it.

Dieting And Mental Barriers

Now that you have been educated on the most common misconceptions, the next step would be to focus on the mental barriers existing on dieting and weight loss. You may have tried certain diets and exercise plans, only to see them fail. This may be because of the psychological block in your way. Weight loss is an uphill battle for any person, but the emotional struggles are certainly different for each individual.

The average person almost always has good intentions when it comes to eating the right foods and exercising on a regular basis. Despite our best intentions, we tend to end up self-sabotaging the progress made. This normally occurs when we are tired, bored, stressed, frustrated, or even sad. Whenever these emotions come up your progress goes back down.

To top it all off, it is likely that you have very good rationalization skills when it comes to convincing yourself to eat badly. Many people have the belief that eating junk foods could provide the relief and comfort you need. You may actually feel better when you eat, and you generally feel better when you eat foods such as sugars and simple carbs.

One of the most common mental barriers is an all-or-nothing kind of mindset. You find yourself treading on a very thin line where your food plan has to be perfect, or you completely fall off the wagon. People expect themselves to succeed or fail. They believe there is no in-between when it comes to weight loss. When you practice this all-or-nothing kind of thinking, you will struggle to return to healthy habits after having a cheat day. This means you will have to start over until the day you actually just give up.

So, focus on developing a more practical mindset. If you fail one day, just carry on with your healthy lifestyle the next. If you eat one unhealthy snack, don't carry on indulging because you have already failed your plan.

The truth of the matter is if you have a negative body image, it can actually hinder your weight loss process. There is generally nothing wrong with improving your health and the appearance you currently have. But, a negative body image is also normally linked to unhealthy eating patterns alongside other problems. Therefore, if you are very self-conscious, you will find yourself overindulging or starving because of your negative body image. Focus on becoming more positive and viewing your body as something to be improved but not something bad.

The most common factor that sets you up for failure is stress. It is impossible not to have stress in life. The problems arise when people use food as a way to calm their emotions. This strategy is certainly not uncommon for any person, but it can create problems if your goal is to lose weight in the long haul. If eating is a way to cope with your stress, it is time to have a change. It is proven that poor choices in what you eat can actually make you feel more anxious. Because you eat the worst foods, you get more stressed, and then you eat more. This is a self-perpetuating cycle that drags you into a whirlwind of dilemmas. Rather, find yourself other calming activities such as meditating or reading that just don't involve food in order to calm yourself down. Exercise is actually a very good stress reliever. That is something you should certainly take into consideration.

Another health issue to consider is depression. Researchers do believe there is a link between depression and unhealthy weight. Even if you are at a healthy weight, if you are depressed it can lead to a lack of appetite and weight loss. Research has suggested that even the perception of being overweight can cause stress and can lead to depression. You might have symptoms such as fatigue and sleeplessness, which can make weight loss more difficult. Certain kinds of antidepressants can cause weight gain as well.

Another common factor that hinders healthy lifestyle changes is self-punishment. Self-punishment does go beyond criticism. Criticism is the normal nagging everyday voice. It tells you you should not eat that or you look horrible in that outfit. Self-punishment is the voice that tells you you're a terrible person and you certainly do not deserve happiness. It is best to work with a therapist if these are some of the things you struggle with. You need to improve your mental health before you can start your weight loss journey.

Putting yourself last is another challenge that you need to learn to overcome. Considering you often have the demands of your job, family, studies, or other circumstances, many things can keep you from exercising and dieting. If you happen to be the main chef at home, it is best to take a stand and introduce fresh and healthy meals. Be confident and involve your kids, spouse, or partner as well. They may actually be surprised with the changes in attitudes, and you will need the support of those close to you. The same thing goes for exercising. Consider scheduling exercise time with your family, whether it is a weekly bike ride, obstacle course, or even going to the gym.

Having a defeatist attitude is another roadblock you may have to overcome. This is when you have an overall negative attitude that brings down your self-esteem and reduces the motivation you need to exercise and make healthy meal choices. Letting this become second nature can certainly help you in your journey.

Overcoming Addictions: Sugar and Caffeine

Having constant cravings for chocolate, candy, or coffee may mean you have an addiction to overcome. It is astounding how far addictions in sugar and caffeine go without being noticed. Yet, a person cannot deny the insatiable craving for sweets and caffeine that come along from time to time. It might also be one of the big struggles to undertake when taking on a new diet. Oftentimes sugar is one of the most egregious factors. Yet it is also wise to cut out a little bit of the caffeine you have in your life. The most common cravings do happen to come from sugar and caffeine; it is one of the bigger mental hurdles to overcome when it comes to dieting.

So why does your brain get addicted to sugar? Your brain actually sees sugar as a reward and it makes you want more of it. This in turn allows you to feel like you need more sugar because you are then the reward when you eat it.

You also get a sugar rush when you eat candy because when you eat the sugar, it converts into a simple form of glucose that is then released into your bloodstream. This allows for your blood sugar to actually spike, which results in your sugar high. However, as quickly as the spike occurred it can crash, therefore forfeiting any benefits that might actually come from sugar. You also tend to feel a pleasurable high when eating sugar, thus making you want more and more. However, the more you carry on repeating this behavior, the more your brain becomes tolerant towards it thus releasing less of the 'high' feelings. So in order to feel the same kind of high as before, you need to increase the frequency and amount. Each and every time you eat sweets, you are hardwiring your brain to crave sugar as well as building up a tolerance. It sounds terrible but the truth remains simple: sugar is addictive and it can be one of your biggest blocks to your weight loss journey.

So how do you overcome this? Here are a few suggestions to break your sugar cravings.

Cutting sugar from your diet could lead to some physical and mental symptoms; everyone has different experiences with withdrawals. Sometimes just sometimes as well as the severity can depend on the amount of sugar you take in through sugary beverages and sweetened foods. Certain people have found some symptoms could potentially last for a few days to even a couple of weeks. However, as soon as your body adapts to a lower sugar diet you will find the symptoms to be less as well as your cravings. However, you could find that the symptoms are worse during specific times of the day. This is even between meals. Stress could even cause certain cravings for sugar and so here are things you need to prepare for.

Firstly you might experience feelings of unhappiness due to a higher lack of endorphins release. You might also find feelings of anxiety as well as restlessness, nervousness, and irritability. You could potentially find changes in your sleep patterns as well as certain cognitive issues. This means you might have difficulty concentrating right after you quit sugar. You will certainly find yourself struggling with cravings and be careful to substitute them with unhealthy foods such as carbohydrates.

Physical symptoms you might experience can include dizziness, lightheadedness, fatigue, and nausea. You might also experience headaches depending upon the severity of the withdrawal symptoms. Giving up on sugar will certainly feel unpleasant but the longer you push yourself the better it will become. Here are some common tips when you cut back on your sugar. You can consider two forms of cutting out your sugar. Firstly you can go cold turkey which is cutting any and all fall out of your diet or make small changes that can affect your overall health. This can certainly help with the withdrawal symptoms as well as with the severity of it.

You can start by swapping out any kind of sugary drinks for water. Once you cut out your fruit juice soda as well as energy drinks you may find yourself losing weight almost immediately. This is because sugary drinks are one of the most common reasons for weight gain. It carries sugar with practically no important nutrients. Secondly, you can start your day with low sugar. So other than eating sugary cereal or even potentially frosted bread you can feel your body with protein which includes eggs as well as vegetables.

You can even add a little bit of sweetness with some fresh fruit or avocado.

You also need to consider reading the labels. Many foods, as well as condiments, sneak sugar into their products. If you read the labels such as salad dressings, opening packets marinara sauce and barbecue sauce you will see it is ripe with added sugar.

Another common obstacle many people have to overcome is the reality of caffeine addiction. Oftentimes people drink caffeine with milk and extra sugar. There are bumps on way too many calories for a person yet they cannot live without it. So you might even want to consider getting a caffeine detox. It also could be leading to certain health problems.

There are two steps you can take when quitting caffeine in a small amount of time. The first step is known as the gradual method. This is actually recommended. with this form, you will quit caffeine gradually. This means you will be reducing the amount of caffeine you consume each and every day. It is based and recommended to step down at least 10 to 30 milligrams every third day until you run out of caffeine completely. This can simply be accomplished by drinking a little less of your normal caffeinated beverage. You can also consider using caffeine tablets; these are great for reducing your caffeine intake in precise increments while also minimizing withdrawal symptoms.

The advantage to this system is that your withdrawal symptoms will be so much less and could potentially be avoided altogether. A person can continue to function as well as be productive and have no caffeine headache to deal with. There will also be less of a shock to the system. However, it can take longer to reduce the amounts depending upon your beginning daily dose. It also does require you to track your calorie intake and be very intentional with how much you drink.

The second method is known as 'cold turkey.' This occurs when you simply stop drinking caffeine all at the same time. This makes it simpler, but it does not make things easier. It is certainly the fastest way you can detox. But it does come at a price, as it will be a huge shock to your body. So it is the fastest way to detox, and you can also realize the heavy influence it can have on your overall functioning.

It can produce quite severe caffeine withdrawal symptoms. A person using this method could potentially be out of commission for one to three days, or even a couple of weeks if their addiction is very severe. It can lead to a loss of productivity and involves a normal habit of giving up just because of how horrible it makes people feel.

If you want to take on the cold turkey method you need to prepare in advance. Here are some steps you can take to make it easier.

Firstly be aware of what caffeine withdrawal or feels like. It is one of the most popular psychoactive substances. Basically, it means it's a stimulant to your nervous system. This affects the neural activity in your brain increasing alertness and reducing fatigue. However, the body does become dependent on caffeine, and eliminating that can cause withdrawal symptoms. Caffeine withdrawal is actually a recognized medical diagnosis. And it can affect anyone who normally and regularly consumes caffeine. You might get headaches which are the most common reported symptoms of caffeine withdrawal. Caffeine can cause the blood vessels to restrict which slows down the blood flow specifically to the brain. So when the sudden change in the blood can cause painful withdrawal and headaches. And it can vary in length and severity as the brain adapts again to the sudden increase in blood. The headaches will cease once the brain has fully adapted to the blood flow.

Secondly, you will struggle with fatigue. Many people actually depend on energy or kick-starting their morning with a single cup of coffee. Because caffeine helps to increase your energy. However, once you remove it can cause the opposite effect with drawbacks such as drowsiness and fatigue.

Another common withdrawal symptom would be anxiety. Caffeine does act as a stimulant that increases your heart rate pressure and adds to your stress hormones. If people are sensitive to caffeine, then one can actually get jittery from just one cup. However, those who withdraw from it have also claimed to become anxious, especially if they had regular caffeine consumption. Additionally, it is best to remember that a lot of caffeine has had milk added to it or sugar. Once you cut out both the coffee and the sugar the withdrawal symptoms can actually be worse.

You may as well stay with a little bit of difficulty in concentrating, considering that the energy drinks coffee and tea boost concentration. So again, with withdrawal, you can struggle with some cognitive functioning.

You may also get a certain level of irritability. It is quite often joked about how coffee drinkers are cranky before their cup of coffee. Yet it is quite often governed by reason of this irritability. The caffeine in coffee only lasts for four to six hours. A person will get the withdrawal symptom of irritability after a night of rest. Therefore, if you drink caffeinated beverages you are likely to become more irritable in the morning. It is difficult for heavy caffeine users to cut back on their caffeine amount without it actually negatively impacting their mood. Another common issue is tremors. These are the ones who have a very serious dependency on caffeine. Tremors are quite severe caffeine withdrawal symptoms. So for people who quit cold turkey from caffeine, it can lead to tremors which should last only two to nine days. If you are experiencing hand tremors longer than that time period then you need to consult the doctor.

Again it is recommended to cut down slowly on your caffeine. Going cold turkey has very severe withdrawal symptoms. So if you are a regular coffee drinker consider switching from regular to decaf. You can alternate from the week after the regular and slowly change it to more and more until you are fully rid of caffeine. The best way and form of dealing with withdrawals is by taking it slow. And being prepared for something like this. Especially if you are taking it cold turkey. It is not recommended but it is important to start cutting bad habits out of one's life. Sugar and caffeine addictions are one of the most common yet unhealthy addictions a person can have. Especially if you want to make changes to your weight loss you need to reconsider the amount of sugar and caffeine consumed. Many of their diets cut out sugar. But they do not focus as much on caffeine.Yet if you add sugar and milk it does make a huge impact, especially if you drink an excessive amount of coffee.

It is also better to avoid sweets in snacks. Granola bars and many protein bars are loaded up with sugar. Choose snacks that are nutrient-dense whole foods like seeds and nuts. You can even consider eating fruit if you have a sweet tooth. This is another way to make sure that the food is not made of sugar.

You also can reconsider having dessert. Whether it is your favorite kind of ice cream or a certain candy bar, you have to consider whether you are actually hungry or you just need a fix of sugar. If you are really hungry, focus on something that is high in protein and fat but not sugar. Having something such as a handful of macadamia nuts or even unsweetened yogurt as well as unsweetened coconut could work.

You can also focus on adapting your whole diet to be nutrient-dense which focuses you and forces you to cut back on added sugar. Not only will you find a decrease in cravings but a decrease in weight as well.

Is recommended to stay hydrated especially when you are suffering from sugar cravings. And it is certainly best and not to drink so that you rather replace it or with water. Make sure to remove any temptation that could be in your house.

Every day you will have to deal with both mental battles from your own side as well as cravings and addictions. It will be a tough journey that tough road and the best you can do for yourself is not to walk on it alone. Find yourself communities for the same goals to keep you accountable. Talk to your family members that you trust as well as to therapists if you need extra help. Keep in mind this journey is a long one. It's no quick-fix. Anyone who tells you differently is trying to sell you something. So strap up and get ready for another amazing journey ahead of you.This is not a short trip. You are in it for the long haul. Again losing weight is not a sprint it is a marathon. So one of the best things you can do for yourself is to accept the reality that it is going to take time, patience, and a lot of mistakes. But it will be all worth it in the end. You might think you don't wanna spend the time on it. Yet as much as you want things to stop, time will not wait for you. It may take two years to overcome everything. You may feel this is too long, but regardless of whether you make those changes or not, time will pass quickly. You will end up thanking yourself in two years time before you even know it.

Overcoming The Odds

Lastly, here are some ideas you can incorporate in order to build for yourself a supportive environment. Firstly, you can be ruthlessly clear about your target goal and why exactly it matters. You need to break down your goal into smaller bite-size pieces in order to make it achievable as well as motivating. Set up a supportive environment in your workplace as well as your home in order to motivate you to carry on. Even removing temptations and adding healthy snacks are two steps closer to overcoming the odds.

Consider sharing your goal with other people to hold you accountable. You are far more likely to watch what you eat if you know you need to tell someone at the end of the day. They can also help you out when you are having your bad days.

Envision how reaching your goal will inevitably make you feel. It is great to imagine yourself in the weight you desire as well as your appearance. Again, be realistic and avoid comparing yourself to celebrities especially in using the Photoshopped figures found in magazines.

Consider your goal as a part of who you are. You are striving towards weight loss and health because you believe yourself to be valuable. Worth the time as well as the investment.

Do keep in mind that you can read as many books as you want but no one will motivate you better than yourself. You are your own greatest enemy as well as your own greatest ally. Prioritizing yourself and your life should be something you consider an everyday thing. When you are eating healthily and not focusing on your overall health you're putting yourself on the back burner. You keep listening to the stories of those who have lost weight and those who have succeeded all come up with the same thing they did not prioritize allows as well. What you need to do is to focus on your overall well-being. As soon as you see a difference in your life your value and self-worth will also grow. Building a balanced weight loss regimen depends entirely upon you and what you decide. There are many steps that you can take. Now that you are here you are certainly far better than most other people. Yet now after you learn about the diets and the steps it will be up to you to follow through and make the changes.

Chapter 3: Keto Diet—Everything You Need To

The keto diet is a low carb, protein moderated, and high-fat diet which is meant to help you burn fat more effectively. It seems self-contradictory that a person should consume fat to lose fat. However, it has proven to have many benefits when it comes to weight loss for women's health. This is the reason why the keto diet has been recommended by many doctors and healthcare professionals.

The keto diet is especially useful when losing excess body fat and also has been proven a good method of reducing your hunger and fighting type 2 diabetes. Therefore it is best to fully understand what a keto diet is, the steps it would involve and why you should consider going for this time.

Keto Diet—What Sets it Apart?

As mentioned at the beginning of the chapter, it is a very low carb but higher fat diet. It shares similarities with many other low-carb diets, but it does have a few differences. When you eat fewer carbs in a keto diet, you do maintain a moderate consumption of protein. You also increase the intake of your fat. When you reduce the carbs you put inside your body you turn your body into a state of ketosis. This is where you burn fat from both your diet and your body for energy.

The term keto or ketogenic is named because it focuses on encouraging your body to produce small fuel molecules. These small fuel molecules are called ketones. They are an alternative fuel source for your body to burn, especially when your blood has a shortage of glucose.

When you cut down the carbs that consume fewer calories, your liver produces the ketones from the fat. These ketones focus on feeding your body and your brain while protecting the protein. Your brain is certainly a very hungry organ. It consumes a lot of calories every single day. However, it cannot use fat directly. You can only run on glucose or ketones. When you are on a ketogenic diet this will cause your body to switch the fuel supply to fat, using fat as its fuel system all day long. Your insulin levels do tend to drop as well as increasing your fat burning. It becomes easier for your body to access your fat stores and burn them off. This is very good if you want to lose weight. It brings alongside other benefits such as less hunger as well as a good supply of energy. This avoids sugar peaks as well as the energy crashes that come with high-calorie meals. A keto diet will help you stay alert, focused, and energized throughout the day.

When your body produces ketones it tends to enter a state in your metabolism that is called ketosis. The quickest way to get into that state is through fasting. This requires not eating anything for a certain amount of time. At times, fasting is not as healthy or comfortable. A keto diet can still trigger ketosis while you are not fasting. It has many of the same benefits that come with fasting, including weight loss.

However, like any other diet or practice, some people are not qualified to take on the ketogenic diet. For most people it is safe, but three groups should reconsider. These are people who have diabetes, those who have medication for high blood pressure, and people who are breastfeeding or pregnant. If you fall within these three categories, it is best to consult with a professional before starting your diet.

Studies with Regard To the Keto Diet

Studies done in Harvard, Campos, 2017, have provided evidence of benefits that have proved keto dieting to be a faster weight loss method in comparison to those who take on the low carb diets or others such as a Mediterranean diet. A review had been set that it can certainly treat certain conditions and even increase the and further boosts the chances of weight loss. However, again it can be quite a difficult diet to follow through on and many people do not tend to stick with this in the long haul.

There have been studies over the long-term effects of a keto diet according to Dashti et al., 2004, where there were a significant decrease in the total level of cholesterol levels as well as reduced body weight and body mass in obese patients. Therefore it shows that people have done the work and research and multiple studies have been given to fully understand the effects of Keto. It is popular for a reason.

Food

There are many foods you can enjoy while on a keto diet, but your carbohydrate intake should not exceed 100 grams, and ideally falls below 50 grams. The fewer carbs you consume, the more effective impact it will have on your entire diet. It might be helpful to start by counting your carbs and stick to keto recipes.

Foods you should consider avoiding are those that contain a high amount of carbs, including sugar and starch. Starchy foods to avoid are rice, pasta, bread, and potatoes. It's also best to avoid foods that have been highly processed. You should also avoid low-fat diet products.

While on a keto diet, water by far is the best drink. Coffee and tea are also acceptable. It is recommended to use no sweeteners, especially regular sugar, in your beverages. Feel free to add a splash of cream, but watch your carb intake, especially if you drink multiple cups of coffee or tea. You can have a glass of wine now and then, but try to avoid alcohol altogether.

Benefits of A Keto Diet

While a keto diet is a dramatic lifestyle change, it also includes many benefits. Ketogenic diets have been proven to be a rapid weight loss technique. Its strategy is to restrict carbs to induce a state of ketosis in your body and reduce body fat, while also increasing muscle mass. Studies have shown that low carb and ketogenic diets have achieved weight loss over a long period. Some have been shown to lose an average of 33 pounds a year. This is approximately six pounds more than what an average low-fat diet has been shown to achieve.

A ketogenic diet has also been shown to stabilize levels of blood sugar because it strictly limits carbohydrate intake. A keto diet can decrease blood sugar spikes. This helps to keep your blood sugar in control, especially if you struggle with high blood sugar. Being able to keep control of your blood glucose levels can reduce the risk of health complications in the long run. It has been proven that ketogenic diets do have additional benefits to people who have type 2 diabetes, not only through the control of blood sugar but also by reducing their dependence on diabetes medication. It has been shown that 95 percent of people were able to reduce or even stop diabetes medication while on a ketogenic diet (Gunnars, 2018). However, if you do want to take on this diet as a type 2 diabetic, you need to consult a doctor. Not only will they be aware of any potential complications in your case, but they will also advise you on the most effective strategy to take on.

It has also been shown that a low-carb diet can reduce your appetite. Hunger is amongst the worst side effects of dieting. It is quite possibly one of the biggest reasons why people give up on their motivation. However, focusing on a reduction in carbs can also lead to a reduction in your appetite. People who cut carbs and eat higher levels of protein and fat tend to eat far less (Gunnars, 2018).

It is also encouraging to know that a great portion of the fat loss comes from your abdominal cavity. Considering that not all the fat in your body is the same, where the fat is stored can also affect your health and risk. There are two kinds of fat. One is known as subcutaneous fat. This is the fat that comes under your skin. The other is known as visceral fat.

Visceral fat forms around a person's organs. It also tends to build up in your abdominal cavity. Typically, this occurs in men, but women are also vulnerable to this form of fat. When there is an excess of visceral fat, it plays a role in insulin resistance and inflammation. It could be the driving cause of dysfunction in the metabolic system of people in western society today. Low-carb diets are supremely effective in reducing harmful visceral fat. It is being shown that the greater portion of fat loss does tend to come from the abdominal cavity. This leads to the reduction of heart disease and type 2 diabetes.

Ketogenic diets have also been shown to dramatically drop triglycerides in the body. Triglycerides are the fat molecules that circulate within your bloodstream. It is a fact that high levels of triglycerides can occur overnight quite quickly. This acts as a strong contributor to heart disease. The issue with elevated triglycerides is that people are consuming too many carbs, especially the simple sugars known as fructose. When people cut their carb intake, they also experience a massive reduction in the triglycerides in their blood. It is shown on the opposite side of the spectrum that low-fat diets tend to increase your triglycerides.

A keto diet also has increased levels of high-density lipoprotein (HDL) cholesterol, which is colloquially known as good cholesterol. It does play a factor in reducing the risk of heart disease as well. Your low-density lipoprotein (LDL) cholesterol, which is known as bad cholesterol, levels will also improve. A ketogenic diet will boost your heart health.

Disadvantages of the Keto Diet

Unfortunately, no diet is perfect. Keto has been shown to have a wide range of health benefits. However, remaining in the ketogenic diet has been shown to have some adverse effects in the long run. It does mean that you could have an increased risk of certain health problems. This simply means that ketogenic diets are meant for a shorter period. This is not something you can adopt permanently.

Firstly, some people have experienced kidney stones, deficiencies in minerals or vitamins, excess protein in the blood, and a build-up of fat in the liver. Some other, more common adverse symptoms include nausea, low tolerance for exercise, constipation, low blood sugar, vomiting, headaches, and fatigue. Many of these symptoms do tend to come along at the very beginning of your diet. This is because your body is adjusting to a brand new energy source. Therefore, if you are struggling with eating disorders or have kidney disease it is best to avoid this diet.

At the end of the day, it is always recommended to discuss your diet plan with a doctor or a dietitian. You should especially discuss switching to a keto diet with your doctor if you struggle with health issues, but everyone should run it by a professional before they start. Because a ketogenic diet does severely restrict the number of carbs to eat you need to be careful, considering there are some carbohydrates that do provide a lot of health benefits. If you want to be less restrictive with the keto diet, you can consume a lot of fibrous and nutrient-dense carbs. These include foods such as fruits and vegetables, in addition to nutritious sources of protein and healthy fats.

It is recommended to take on a keto diet for a couple of weeks or months. You could potentially extend up to two years, however, it is best not to push your limits too far. Try to keep it to a couple of months and transition it back to a less restrictive diet which you can maintain for the long term. Consider a good ketogenic diet to kickstart your weight loss journey.

Chapter 4: Keto Diet -Recipes to Try

If you are interested in the Keto diet, then it does make sense whether or not you would like to try out some recipes. Even if you do not want to take on the full diet, there is nothing wrong with doing a little experimenting or a test trial on whether or not you might enjoy this diet form.

Recipe 1: Creamy Tuscan Garlic Chicken

Firstly, you can try a creamy Tuscan Garlic chicken. It is in an amazing garlic sauce with spinach and sun-dried tomatoes. You can have it ready in about 30 minutes.

You will need:

- 1 ½ pound boneless and skinless chicken breasts.
- 2 tablespoons olive oil
- 1 teaspoon salt
- 1 cup heavy cream

- ½ cup chicken broth
- 1 teaspoon garlic powder
- ½ cup of parmesan cheese
- 1 teaspoon Italian seasoning
- ½ cup sun-dried tomatoes
- 1 cup spinach

First, you will need to cook the chicken. Use a large skillet and add olive oil. Cook chicken on medium-high heat for 3 to 5 minutes on each side until brown. Make sure it is no longer pink in the center. Remove the chicken and set it aside.

Secondly, you need to whisk together the cream sauce. Add to the cream garlic powder, chicken broth, parmesan cheese, and Italian seasoning. Immediately start whisking over medium-high heat until it reaches a point of thickening. Then add the spinach as well as the sun-dried tomatoes and allow to simmer until the spinach starts to wilt.

Lastly, combine the chicken and the sauce. You do this by adding the chicken back to the pan and serving.

Recipe 2: Baked Eggs with Zoodles and Avocado

Try your hand at ketogenic baked eggs alongside zoodles with avocado. This recipe will be ready in about 20 minutes.

You will need:

- nonstick spray
- 3 zucchini, spiralized
- 2 tbsp extra-virgin olive oil
- kosher salt and freshly ground black pepper
- 4 large eggs
- 2 avocados, sliced
- red pepper flakes
- fresh basil

Preheat the oven to 350 degrees. Spray the baking sheet with a nonstick spray. In a large bowl, add the zucchini noodles and olive oil. Season it with pepper and salt. Then, divide it into four equal portions and place it on the baking sheet. Shape it into a nest.

Crack an egg in the center of each noodle nest. Bake until the eggs are fully set, about 9 to 11 minutes. Season with salt, pepper, red pepper flakes, and basil. Serve alongside avocado slices.

Recipe 3: Cheesy Cauliflower Breadsticks

These are gluten-free cheese and cauliflower breadsticks you can try. These take about 1 hour 30 minutes to prepare.

You will need:

- 1 head of cauliflower which is cut
- 2 garlic clove pieces
- 2 eggs, beaten lightly
- ⅓ cup mozzarella cheese, shredded
- ⅓ cup Parmesan cheese, grated
- 1 egg white
- 1 tbsp fresh thyme, chopped
- 1 tbsp fresh rosemary chopped
- Salt and ground pepper
- 2 tbsp extra-virgin olive oil

First, preheat the oven to 425°. Line a baking sheet with some parchment paper. Then in a food processor bowl, combine the cauliflower florets and garlic. Pulse it until it resembles a fine meal for about 3 minutes. Transfer it to a large mixing bowl. Add mozzarella, parmesan cheese, eggs, and rosemary into the cauliflower, making sure it's well-combined. Season it with some salt and pepper. Press the cauliflower mixture into a half-inch thick circle on the baking sheet. Brush with the olive oil and bake it until it's crisp and golden on the edges for about 25 to 30 minutes. Cool it for 45 minutes before slicing it into sticks and serving.

Recipe 4: Prosciutto & Cauliflower Bites

These are delicious crispy prosciutto-wrapped cauliflower bites. This makes a great snack or appetizer, especially at holiday get-togethers. These take around 20 minutes.

You need:

- 1 small cauliflower head
- Half cup of tomato paste
- 2tspb white wine
- ½ tsp black pepper
- ½ cup of grated parmesan cheese
- 20 slices of prosciutto
- 6 tbsp of olive oil

First, you need to prepare the cauliflower head by cutting off the base of the cauliflower, including the green leaves. Cut it in half and cut the halves into 1-inch thick slices, and then into two or three bite-sized pieces. Bring a large pot of salted water to a boil. Blanch cauliflower in the water until it is almost tender, about 3 minutes. Then pat it dry with paper towels.

Combine tomato paste, pepper, and white wine in a small bowl, mixing well. Then, take one teaspoon of the paste mixture and spread it on the sides of each cauliflower. Sprinkle parmesan and gently wrap a slice of prosciutto all around each piece of cauliflower. Make sure it is secure at the ends by pressing it.

Working in batches, heat 2 tablespoons of olive oil over in a large skillet. Use medium heat. Make sure the oil is hot before adding the cauliflower and cook it until the prosciutto is golden and crisp. This should take around 3-4 minutes. Serve and enjoy!

Recipe 5: Keto Broccoli Salad

This salad makes a great lunch, especially when prepared in advance! This takes about 10 minutes to make.

You will need:

- Kosher salt
- 3 broccoli heads, cut into small bite-sizes
- ¼ red onion which is thinly sliced
- ¼ cup toasted and sliced almonds
- 3 slices of bacon which is cooked and crumbled
- 2tbs freshly chopped chives
- ½ cups of shredded Cheddar

For the dressing, you will need

- Kosher salt
- ⅔ cups of mayonnaise
- 3 tablespoons of apple cider vinegar
- 1 tablespoon of dijon mustard
- freshly ground black pepper

First, bring 6 cups of salted water to boil in a medium pot or saucepan. While you wait, prepare a large bowl of ice water.

Add broccoli florets into the boiling water and let it cook until it is soft and tender. This takes 1-2 minutes. Remove with a slotted spoon and place it in the ice bowl. When it is cool, drain the florets in a colander.

Get a medium bowl and whisk all the dressing ingredients together, seasoning with some salt and pepper.

Combine all the salad ingredients inside a large bowl and start pouring the dressing. Toss and mix everything until it is fully coated in the dressing. Refrigerate it until it is ready to be served.

Recipe 6: Keto Meatballs in Sauce

Add these meatballs to a keto-friendly pasta substitute for a great dinner. These take about 25 minutes to prepare.

You will need:

- 1 pound of ground beef
- 1 garlic clove, minced
- ½ cup of shredded mozzarella
- ¼ cup of grated parmesan
- 2 tablespoons of chopped parsley
- 1 egg, beaten
- 1 teaspoon of kosher salt
- ½ teaspoon of black pepper freshly ground
- 2 tablespoons of extra-virgin olive oil

For the sauce you will need:

1 medium-sized onion, chopped
2 garlic cloves minced
1 can of crushed tomatoes
1 teaspoon of dried oregano
kosher salt
fresh ground black pepper

First, get a large bowl and combine the beef, garlic, parmesan, mozzarella, egg, parsley, salt, and pepper. Shape it into 16 meatballs.

Then, get a large skillet and heat the oil over medium heat. Add the meatballs and cook them, turning them now and then until all sides of the meatballs are golden brown. This takes about 10 minutes. Remove the skillet from heat and place the meatballs on a paper towel-lined plate.

In the same skillet, add the onions and saute for about 5 minutes. Add the garlic and cook for 1 minute more. Add the tomatoes as well as the oregano and season it with salt and pepper.

Finally, add the meatballs into the sauce and let the sauce cover, and simmer over it until it thickens. This takes about 15 minutes. You can add some extra parmesan before you serve it.

Chapter 5: Diet Types—Paleo, Vegan, Low Carb, and Blood Type Diets

Now that you have looked at the keto diet, you might be curious to find out more about other healthy weight loss diets. Considering each diet has its unique benefits. It would be best to have a good understanding of all the options you have for your weight loss journey. It is not all about weight loss; it is also about improving and boosting your health and eating in a way that you can enjoy. Some people cannot live without carbs or enjoy carbs. This means it would be quite impractical for them to embrace a ketogenic diet. However, that does not mean that they cannot go on a different diet. You need to decide what sounds most appealing and practical for your everyday life.

Paleo Diet Explained

A paleo diet is a dietary plan based on foods similar to what was eaten in the paleolithic era. The paleo diet includes foods such as fruits and vegetables, lean meats, fish, and nuts, and seeds. All of these foods could have been obtained through hunting and gathering in ancient times. It limits the foods to common farming. Other names for the paleo diet are the hunt-gather or Stone age diets.

The purpose of the paleo diet is to change eating habits back to the way that people have eaten in earlier eras of human history. The reasoning is that our bodies are not matched or created for the modern diets that have emerged. It is believed that this mismatch is one of the huge factors that contribute to obesity, diabetes, and other diseases that plague humanity today. The reason why you may consider a paleo diet is because you want to lose weight or maintain a healthy weight.

Paleo Diet: Benefits and Drawbacks

Several advantages come because of the paleo diet. The diet is rich in potassium, considering you will be eating a lot of vegetables and fruit. Potassium helps your body maintain healthy blood pressure and healthy kidney and muscle function.

The fats in a paleo diet are also quite healthy. This diet includes a healthy amount of unsaturated fats. These are normally found in nuts, avocados, and olive oil.

A paleo diet is also very high in protein, which your body uses for the growth and development of muscles, bones, and cartilage. Having a good amount of lean protein can certainly help contribute to your body's overall health.

Embracing the paleo diet will also mean eliminating processed foods. These are foods that have been inundated with chemicals to make them last longer and taste better. Eliminating this from your diet will keep you from consuming salt and sugar in excessive amounts. This will improve your blood sugar and reduce the risks of cardiovascular disease and diabetes.

However, there are also drawbacks to the paleo diet. The food portions allowed in the diet do not reach the recommended daily allowances. You will also be eliminating entire food groups. Does that mean you can miss out on essential nutrients or vitamins? Considering most people obtain calcium from milk, yogurt, or cheese, they might find themselves running on a calcium shortage and lower bone and tooth density.

If you also eliminate whole grain, your fiber intake will be lower. That means there will be a decrease in your gut health. The diet does not take into consideration the wide range of foods that are now available in the modern-day and age and could potentially be inadequate in comparison to what your body needs. It is not possible to adopt the same diet everyone ate in the paleolithic era. Therefore, it is best to customize your paleo diet to the nutrition that you need. You can follow a paleo diet if you make sure you eat enough foods to increase your calorie intake and get the nutrition they need. Certain deficiencies can cause permanent damage, so it is critical to make sure that no matter what diet you follow, you get the nutrients you need. After all, diets are meant to boost your health, not worsen it.

Paleo Diet: Steps to Take

Here are things you need to eat:

- vegetables and fruits
- fish (rich in omega 3)
- nuts and seeds
- lean meats (those from grass-fed animals or wild game)
- oils that come from nuts and fruits (olive oil, sunflower seed oil, etc.)

Foods to avoid are:

- Refined sugar

- Salt
- Legumes (beans, lentils, peanuts, and peas)
- Potatoes
- Grains
- Highly processed foods
-

A normal day's meals could look like cantaloupe and some broiled salmon for breakfast, salad and lean pork for lunch, steamed broccoli salad with lean beef for dinner, and strawberries for dessert. For snacks, you could have orange, celery sticks, or even carrot sticks.

Vegan Diet Explained

Vegan diets have gained a lot of popularity recently. Many people have decided to go vegan for ethical, health, and environmental reasons. When a vegan diet is done correctly, it can result in many health benefits. This does include weight loss and improved blood sugar. However, considering that a vegan is a purely plant-based diet, there is a risk of nutrient deficiencies.

Veganism is described as a way to live that excludes any form of animal exploitation or cruelty. Veganism not only includes food but also clothing and other products. As a vegan, your diet is certainly devoid of any products that come from animals. This includes dairy eggs and honey. There are a vast range of reasons why people become vegan. However, there is a common stem of improved health that comes with being a vegan. There are different kinds of vegan diet forms. The most common is a wholly vegan diet. These diets focus on plant foods such as legumes, whole grains vegetables, fruits, nuts, and seeds.

Another common vegan diet is a raw vegan diet. This diet is made up of raw vegetables, fruits, and other plant products that are cooked at or below 180 degrees Fahrenheit.

There is the 80/10/10 diet. This is a raw vegan diet that restricts the amount of fat and focuses on raw foods and soft greens. Is also known as a low-fat vegan diet. The diet is based on the idea that it needs at least 80 percent of the calories from complex carbs whereas it needs about 10 percent from protein and the other 10 percent from fats according to Petre, 2017. It doesn't have a time limit and has been promoted to increase longevity as well as reduce obesity.

Then there is the raw till 4 diets. It is inspired by the 80/10/10 but does have a starch solution. The rule is that raw foods are eaten until 4-o'clock. Then, a person has the option to have a cooked vegan meal in the evening.

Another similar diet is the starch solution. This is when you have a high-carb vegan diet that focuses on starches that are cooked instead of food.

Another common but funny form of the vegan diet is the junk vegan diet. This is a diet that lacks in whole plant foods but rather relies heavily on alternative cheeses meat vegan desserts and fries. All of these tend to be heavily processed vegan foods.

There are multiple variations of a vegan diet, but there are not many differences between the varieties. Rather, it depends on your choice as a vegan when it comes to preferences.

Do not mistake a vegan diet for a vegetarian. Vegetarians do not eat meat like a vegan, but they do consume dairy and cheese products normally.

Vegan Diet: Benefits and Drawbacks

It has been generally shown that vegans do tend to have a lower body mass index. This is why people tend to turn to vegan diets to lose weight. Vegans tend to add healthier life choices alongside their meals.

Vegan diets are more effective for weight loss than an average diet method. Due to the focus on the products, you actually may and may not consume. Additionally, there is less of a restriction on the amounts you need to eat, because of the lower calories in vegan meals. Even if people eat until they are full as a vegan, they are more likely to eat less because of the higher fiber intake than if you were to eat as a non-vegan. All in all, you may just automatically eat fewer foods as well as eat more complex and healthier foods.

It has been shown that adopting the vegan diet can have a positive effect on your blood sugar. It can even keep type 2 diabetes at bay. Studies have shown that veganism lowers blood sugar levels and increases insulin sensitivity.

As a vegan, your heart will also be kept far more healthy than if you were consuming animal meals. It lowers the risk of developing high blood pressure by 75percent and reduces the risk of dying of heart disease by as much as 42percent (Petre, 2016). If you become a vegan, you may find your cholesterol and blood sugar also reducing. This plays an impact on the reduction of risk towards heart disease.

Other benefits that have been discovered are a reduction in cancer. Vegans do benefit from a decreased risk of up to 5% from developing or dying of cancer according to Wholesome Culture, 2018.

Arthritis and its symptoms have been shown to decrease when taking on a vegan diet. These include pain, swelling of the joints, and morning stiffness. It can certainly help to turn you more into an early bird.

The vegan diet also plays a role in the function of your kidneys. Substituting meat for plant protein could again reduce the risks of having poor kidney function.

Studies have furthermore shown that as a vegan you are reducing risks of developing Alzheimer's disease according to Wholesome Culture, 2018.

However, the benefits of a vegan lifestyle transcend physical wellbeing. Veganism helps the environment as well.

Veganism has the power to combat world hunger. A lot of food that is grown is not eaten by humans; 70% of the grain which is grown in the United States is used to feed livestock and 3% of farmland is specifically set aside for animal food.

Meat does contain more calories than plants, but there are plenty of nutrients within plants. Furthermore, going vegan can certainly help stop the deforestation, pollution, and overfishing caused by the production and harvesting of animal products.

Going vegan also conserves water. There are so many people around the world that do not have access to clean water. Others struggle with scarcity due to drought or abuse of water sources. Farming livestock consumes more freshwater than almost anything else. The agricultural farmlands are also one of the biggest pollutants on the planet. To put it simply, a pound of beef can take about 100 to 200 times more water than a pound of plants. Just cutting down on a single pound of beef could save 15,000 gallons of water. So even if you do not consider veganism, maybe skip out on a meaty meal every once in a while.

Becoming a vegan could potentially help with cleansing soil. Just as livestock have pollution to the water, they also play a role in erosion and soil pollution. This is because the raising of livestock requires deforestation and land. Deforestation is still accelerating each year, it will have devastating effects in the long term.

Lastly, another benefit of veganism is the fact that it has a positive impact on the air we breathe. Agricultural farming contributes to greenhouse gas emissions. Reducing the amount of demand coming from cows and sheep would reduce the pollution in the air.

Keep in mind many of the studies on the health benefits of veganism have been anecdotal. This means that although it applies to some people, others may not necessarily receive all these benefits. Again, there is no perfect diet for everybody. Rather, it is best to tailor and choose the diet that best suits you.

There are some issues when going vegan that people need to be aware of. Many of these are preventable in a vegan diet, but one needs to be aware of them.

Firstly, many vegans do happen to struggle with vitamin B12 deficiencies because B12 is only naturally found in animal products. Vitamin B12 deficiencies can cause permanent nerve damage. It is best to stock up on some vegan supplements to prevent this from happening.

Vitamin D deficiency is also quite common, so getting supplements or basking for 15 minutes a day in the sun will help solve this problem for you.

Many plant-based foods do contain iron, but your body may struggle to absorb it from the plant source. So you do need to include a lot (add some vitamin C-rich plant food alongside it) and take supplements if you are aware that you are not consuming enough.

Considering that iodine is found naturally in seafood, you can get a slight deficiency from this nutrient. The best step you can take is by getting yourself some iodized salt to make 100percent sure you are getting iodine in your meal.

Selenium is also commonly found in fish. This is why you need to consider adding Brazil nuts into your diet. They are extremely rich in this mineral, and just eating one per day will satisfy your nutritional needs.

Lastly, you may struggle with Omega 3 Fatty Acids. They are normally found in fish, but you can certainly opt for the vegan supplement or even the vegan-friendly choice of algae oil.

The best you can do for yourself to start off as a vegan is to build yourself a well-thought-out and structured meal plan. Many of these deficiencies and issues can simply be avoided with a proper plan at your doorstep. Not only can it act as a helping hand and guide, but you learn what you are actually putting in your body and the benefits you gain from every meal.

Low Carb Diet Explained

Low-carb diets are self-explanatory. They are diets that limit carbohydrates. Those are normally found in grains, vegetables, and fruits. Rather, you would focus on foods very high in protein and fat. They are very similar to a keto diet, but a little less restrictive. Low-carb diets are normally chosen for weight loss, but some health benefits extend beyond weight loss.

Choosing a low-carb diet will help you lose weight, change your bad eating habits and allow yourself to enjoy a different variety of foods you may have never even considered trying out before.

In a low-carb diet, it is better to restrict the simpler carbs. These are refined carbs such as table sugar. Focus on consuming carbs that are complex and natural. Such as wheat flour, milk, legumes, grains, fruits, veggies, and seeds. Complex carbs are digested far more slowly and have a smaller impact on the overall blood sugar in your body in comparison to refined carbs. They also provide a healthy dose of fiber, which is beneficial for your gut health.

Do keep in mind that sugars and white loaves of bread are considered processed foods as well as refined carbs. Other refined carbs are pasta, cookies, candy, cake, and even sodas and drinks that have high sugar content.

Considering that your body does use carbs as your main energy source, the carbs are broken down into simple sugars and afterward are simply released into your blood. This is known as blood glucose. It is up to the insulin to release the glucose in the blood cells or have it stored in the liver as well as the muscle. When this occurs, your body converts these carbs into fats. Focusing on a low-carb diet allows the body to start burning the stored fat for energy leading to inevitable weight loss.

Much like keto, your main sources of food should be protein and non-starchy veggies. You should normally limit the number of grains, pieces of bread, sweets, pasta, and starchy vegetables as well as your seeds and nuts. But unlike Keto, there is a certain level of them allowed. You can consider restricting less every day or consider making alternative days where you are stricter on the carbs than others. Or you can start by greatly restricting the number of carbs and gradually increasing it as time goes by.

The dietary guidelines for carbs, however, are recommended for 45percent-65percent, so make sure you keep your carbs between 900-1,300 calories.

Low Carb Diet: Benefits and Drawbacks

Weight loss is an obvious benefit. It will already happen for you considering there is a restriction in certain calories, and the weight loss will be better yet if you do increase your physical activity. Very low carb diets could lead to faster weight loss over the short term, but it is best again to stick to these diets between 12-24 months.

You may experience some drawbacks such as constipation, headaches, and even muscle cramps. This is to do with your body adapting to a new diet, but if the symptoms should persist you need to consult with a professional and consider placing your diet on a halt.

Blood Type Diet

Likely, you have never considered having a diet based on your blood type, but such a diet exists and was designed by Peter J. D'Adamo who made claims that your body reacts to the food you eat through your blood type (Watson, 2013). It is thought that your blood type does digest certain foods better than others, thus focusing on those can help you lose weight as well as increase certain health aspects.

Advantages and Disadvantages of Blood Type Diet

Firstly, exercise is normally encouraged when taking on the blood type diet. Anyone knows that despite how difficult it may be, exercise always tends to work in your favor and brings along many health advantages all on its own. When you exercise and eat well it certainly does lead to weight loss and having a good grip on weight management. Do keep in mind no research has truly been done in regards to any added benefits of the blood type diet and exercise.

Every blood type diet does specifically focus on whole foods in comparison to processed foods. No matter what or where this is always a healthy choice by far. The different diets also have a wider variety, thus making it far more flexible for other people to stick with and use in their everyday lives.

It does come with its fair share of restrictions, yet it is not known to be unusually healthy in regards to one's calorie intake. This is already a blessing in disguise and many diets can place you in starvation mode if you are not careful. This leads to loss of muscle rather than fat and a slower metabolism. The plans for the blood types, specifically type B and AB are known to be actually covering most if not all the nutrients your body needs in order to survive and thrive.

However, this diet has not had any extensive research done on it so far. There are certain questionnaires and analyses that have been done proving that the diets for blood type A and Ab certainly lowered cholesterol levels and a diet close to blood type's O actually had a lowered level of triglycerides, but there is nothing truly set in stone according to https://www.facebook.com/verywell, 2021.

So ultimately keep in mind that following this diet form is more on the foundation of a theory, but never truly proven. However, one cannot deny the reality that what this diet form truly emphasizes will make your meals healthier, thus making weight loss through this diet plan not too much of a far-fetched idea.

Blood Type Diets: Foods For Each Type

If you have blood type O then you need to consider focusing on a heavy-protein-based diet. This normally does consist of having poultry, fish, lean meats as well as vegetables. It is then recommended that you limit the amount of dairy, grains, and beans that you eat as well as add a certain amount of supplements to deal with stomach issues people with this blood type have a habit of getting.

If you have Type B blood then it is recommended to avoid buckwheat, tomatoes, lentils, corn, wheat, peanuts, and even sesame seeds. You may also find that chickens could cause problems and rather focus on having certain meats, eggs, vegetables, and low-fat dairy.

If you have type A blood then focusing on a meat-free diet is the recommended way to go. Rather focus on your vegetables and fruits and it is best to keep it organic. This is because D'Adamo has made certain claims that those who have type A tend to have a more sensitive immune system.

Lastly, if you have type AB blood then you need to eat dairy, tofu, green vegetables, and seafood. It is claimed that having this blood type means you have lower acidity in your stomach, and it is best to avoid or limit your alcohol, caffeine, and any meat that has been cured or smoked.

Here are a few things to remember, that you'll have to normally take a blood test in order to find out your blood type, and certain blood type diets can actually be majorly restricting. Your blood type will also affect the choices you make when eating out as well as the foods you purchase. It doesn't give much room for personal preferences but does recommend taking on exercises based on your specific blood type. For someone who has type O, it is recommended to cycle or jog. Type As are recommended to take on tai chi or yoga.

D'Adamo also tends to recommend specialty foods that can take a bite out of your wallet. So before diving into a diet like this, make sure your budget can also fit it in.

However, because this diet takes into consideration what you should eat due to your blood type, it completely excludes any chronic condition such as diabetes. Your blood type diet may tell you to eat high protein yet if you have diabetes it is possible that you shouldn't eat dairy or chicken. If you do have chronic conditions anyhow it is best to take a more practical approach to your eating habits and to be cautious. Consulting with a professional can save you a lot of pain and even potential trips to the hospital. so keep all this in mind when taking on a new diet.

When it comes to dieting, you need to make sure that you are absolutely comfortable and happy with the results that do come your way. If you find yourself very uncomfortable and hungry, then you are doing something wrong. Certain diets are just not meant for certain people. If you see some pretty big drawbacks, or you are not losing the weight you desire, put a pin in that particular diet and work on something else. You need to pick one that should hopefully suit your preferences. If you are not even enjoying the food you need to eat, then you are bound to give up.

Chapter 6: Diet Types: Dukan, Atkins, Intermittent Fasting

The vast variety of diets that are available allow people to choose something that will work. It may take time, and sometimes it may not work. But, that is the beauty of trying out different things. You will get to try out lots of new things. There is no rule that you should not customize the different diets to suit you. Just make sure you are getting the different nutrients necessary.

Dukan Diet Explained

The Dukan diet is a high-protein and low-carb plan designed by a man called Pierre Dukan. He was a French physician and is a self-proclaimed nutritionist. The Dukan method is a diet based on how hunters and gatherers may have eaten in ancient days. The diet includes approximately 100 foods, all of them being proteins or vegetables. A person can eat as much as they possibly want, however they can only stick to those hundred foods. The Dukan diet can contribute to weight loss, but there is research to show that sometimes taking on the diet can cause some complications.

The Dukan diet has the requirements for a person to eat high protein foods as well as reduce the number of carbs and fats, meaning a person prioritizes the amount of protein while focusing on natural foods. Taking on the Dukan Diet also encourages you to have more daily physical activity.

There is an official Dukan website that allows you to see the list of 100 foods. Out of all the hundred foods, there are approximately 68 that are known as pure proteins and 32 that are listed as vegetables. A person can actually introduce other foods during the later stages of a diet. The theory behind the Dukan diet is that focusing on protein can cause weight loss. The reasoning behind this is that lean high protein foods do have a lower calorie count. People have also been more satiated after eating protein. It is known that digesting protein can create more energy, so your body burns more calories.

The Dukan diet is split into four different phases. The first phase is the attack phase. The attack phase focuses on eating foods from the list of pure proteins. However, it does also mean eating fewer calories. Generally, dietitians do agree that no food is the base to kickstart your metabolism. However, taking on a little bit of exercise can. Eating a lot of lean protein and exercising will increase your metabolism, triggering rapid weight loss. The other reasons why people lose weight during this phase are the reduction of carbs and water weight. This phase normally lasts 2 to 5 days. However, some people who intend to lose more than 40 pounds would stay longer in this phase for a maximum of seven days.

In this phase, people can only eat the foods that are on the 68 pure proteins list. These are all lean sources of protein, including items such as beef, chicken, and cottage cheese. All these choices are for certain low in fat and contain no sugars. People on this diet can eat as much as they want because with this diet there is no calorie counting.

This diet includes a rule of eating 1.5 tablespoons of oat bran each and every day, which is known to be very high in fiber. The body cannot break down or digest most of this carbohydrate. The higher fiber does help to suppress your hunger. It is also required for a person to drink about 51 fluid ounces of water a day and to exercise for 20 minutes. This is to help kickstart your attack phase, as well as get things moving in the realm of weight loss.

The second phase is known as the cruise phase. This occurs when you gradually add 32 vegetables into your diet. This means you should alternate between pure protein as well as protein and vegetable days. The length of the space entirely depends upon the amount of weight a person wants to lose. You should consider it to be a pound for every three days. Again, there is no calorie limit to this meal plan.

A person is allowed to eat as much low-fat protein or non-starchy vegetables that they want to. However, everything good is in moderation as the saying goes. At this point, you need to be eating two tablespoons of oat bran and exercising 30 to 60 minutes every day.

The third phase is known as the consolidation phase. This is when you're not to lose weight, but to avoid regaining it by introducing some starchy foods into their diet. Every day a person can eat unlimited quantities of vegetables and protein that are on the list. They are allowed to eat one piece of fruit, two slices of whole-grain bread, and 1.5 ounces of cheddar cheese a day. The Dukan diet also allows one celebration meal each week in this phase. When it comes to the celebration meal, you can eat whatever you want. This phase does require you to have at least one day of the core protein. It is preferable that you pick the same day every week. Be sure to exercise 25 minutes a day.

The last phase is known as the stabilization phase. This is considered a long-term plan. A person should not lose or gain any weight while at this point. One day each week, have an all-protein day. Other than that, you can eat whatever you want as long as you eat three tablespoons of oat bran a day. Take the stairs as often as you can and exercise for 20 minutes every day. Continue to drink 51 ounces of water a day and incorporate all these habits into your lifestyle. The stabilization of the Dukan diet is meant to keep you healthy without too much stress. It is certainly less restrictive than all the other diets when it is completed.

Dukan Diet: Benefits and Drawbacks

Research has proven that this is not the healthiest form of weight loss. High protein diets promote weight loss because it helps to reduce the amount which people eat. It has also been shown to improve the balance of glucose in one's body and to reduce the levels of the hunger hormone called ghrelin. However, because of the limits of certain food groups such as grains and fruits, it does mean it is not a nutritionally complete diet. It can also be quite a difficult and inconvenient form of eating. It is possible to eat out but, certainly very difficult to control when our food is prepared in the restaurants. The Dukan diet has many rules, which can make things difficult to maintain, especially if there are other people in the house who are not following the same diet as you.

The initial weight loss will only be water weight, so it is temporary. Lean proteins can be quite expensive and the rules are quite strict, so it is certainly something you will struggle with for the long term. If people don't stick to the rules they might have an increased risk of long-term health problems.

Studies have also shown that taking on the Dukan diet for too long has certain health risks. These are risks of contracting kidney, liver, cardiovascular disease, and osteoporosis. It should not be a long-term diet. However, once you are up to the final phase, it should generally not be a problem. Some diets are meant to be beneficial for the short term. Others, such as veganism, can remain in the long haul.

It prevents you from rebounding or regaining the weight that you have initially lost and teaches you long-term commitments. Therefore, a person has to decide whether or not they're willing to take on certain of these risks as well as preparing for them. If you seem to be suffering from any symptoms of deficiency then it is time to either get a supplement or visit a professional doctor. It is best to determine which nutrients you are lacking when taking on the diet.

Atkins Diet

The Atkins diet is very low-carb and a popular eating plan that was created in the 1960s. It was designed by cardiologist Robert C. Atkins. The Atkins diet focuses on heavily restricting carbs and emphasizing proteins and fats. It is similar to the Dukan and keto diets, however, the Atkins diet has several phases of weight loss as well as maintenance. It starts out with a very low-carb eating plan but slowly builds its way up. The purpose of the Atkins diet is to change a person's eating plans and habits, as well as helping people to lose weight and keep it off. There are many who claim that the Atkins diet is that healthy and lifelong approach to eating, whether or not you want to lose weight, increase your energy, or improve certain health problems you may have, such as high blood pressure or metabolic syndrome.

There are several reasons why people choose this form of diet. Its main focus is eating the right amount of carbohydrates, proteins, and fat in order to lose weight and keep optimal health. According to the Atkins diet, the reason for obesity and health problems is because of the low fat and high carb diet that is offered worldwide. A person doesn't need to avoid the fatty cuts of meat. They also don't need to trim off all the excess fat that comes in certain foods. It is rather more important to control the number of carbohydrates you receive.

The Atkins diet does have a claim that if you eat too many carbs, specifically sugar and flour, you will have blood sugar imbalances, constant weight gain, and cardiovascular problems. This is why the Atkins diet restricts carbs and encourages more protein and fat intake. However, it does not claim to be a high protein diet. This is where it differs from the Dukan diet. This diet form encourages people to eat high-fiber vegetables and can accommodate those who are vegetarian or even vegan. It addresses the common health problems that arrive in a normal low-carb diet.

Unlike many other diets, the Atkins diet does not require calorie counting or portion control. It does, however, require you to track your carbs. It uses a system called net carbs, which allows you to calculate your carbohydrate intake minus fiber. For instance, four ounces of raw broccoli has a total of 2.3 grams of carbohydrates and 1.3 grams of fiber. Therefore, it places the total net carb value at 1 gram.

The Atkins diet does claim that the approach you take to carbs will certainly help burn the fat stores in your body. It should also help you regulate your blood sugar and help you to achieve the health you desire. It also claims that it won't leave you hungry or deprived of food. Once you have reached your goal weight it can certainly help you identify the tolerance of your carbs. This is by figuring out the number of grams you can certainly eat each day without having to gain or lose weight.

The Atkins diet also claims that exercise is not a crucial element to weight loss. But it does acknowledge it helps with certain health benefits as well as maintaining weight. There are four phases of the Atkins diet, the length of which depends on your weight loss goals.

The first phase is the induction phase. This is the most strict phase where you cut as many carbs out of your diet as it can. You will only be eating 20 grams of net carbs a day. And this mostly comes from vegetables. Instead of getting the typical 45 to 65 percent of calories from carbs, you will only get 10 percent. The foundation of your diet will consist mostly of vegetables such as cucumber, asparagus, celery broccoli, green beans, and peppers. This should make up about 12 to 15 grams. You should eat enough protein such as fish, poultry, shellfish, eggs, cheese, and meat at every single meal. You really don't have to restrict the number of oils or fats, but you certainly cannot have most fruits, bread, sugary baked goods, grains, nuts, or alcohol. Make sure to drink eight glasses of water a day. This phase lasts for at least two weeks, depending upon the amount of weight you want to lose.

The second phase is known as balance. You will continue to eat a minimum of 12 to 15 net carbs. You will also carry on avoiding foods that have added sugar. In this phase, you slowly add certain nutrient-rich carbs such as vegetables, berries, seeds, and nuts. You will continue to lose weight until you are 10 pounds from your goal weight.

The third phase is known as pre-maintenance. In this phase, you will gradually start increasing the range of foods you can eat. This does include starchy vegetables, fruits, and whole grains. You can add an increased amount of 10 grams of net carbs each week. But you have to cut back if you realize your weight is increasing again. You will carry on staying in this phase until you reach your goal weight.

The last phase is known as lifetime maintenance. You will move into this phase as soon as you reach your ideal weight and carry on eating like this for the rest of your life. This is meant to help maintain your weight so that you do not lose or gain any more than necessary.

Here is an example of a common menu for this diet. For breakfast, a person may have scrambled eggs with sauteed onions. Some of the beverages you could drink besides water are coffee, tea, diet soda, or herbal teas. For lunch, you could have chicken alongside a salad with bacon and avocado dressing. For dinner, you could have a baked salmon steak, arugula salad, and asparagus with cherry tomatoes and cucumbers. And for snacks, you can certainly consider eating Atkins products such as a chocolate shake, cheddar cheese, or a granola bar.

Atkins: Benefits and Drawbacks

Generally, an Atkins diet can help you lose up to 15 pounds within the first two weeks. The initial weight you will lose is water weight. You will continue to lose weight in phases two and three as long as you do not eat an excess of carbs.

Most people can actually lose weight on a diet plan that restricts calories, at least in the short term. However, over the long term, the Atkins diet is not as effective as some other weight-loss diets. This is because carbs provide half of the calories that are consumed.

Some of the most common benefits of the Atkins diet are that it can prevent as well as improve some serious health conditions such as metabolic syndrome, high blood pressure, diabetes, and even cardiovascular disease. It may also improve your blood cholesterol and blood sugar levels. There will also be improved levels of triglycerides and better heart health overall. However, there are no major benefits found in the Atkins diet that makes it stand out from several other diets.

So, at the end of the day, it comes back to the point of preference. If the Atkins diet is not working for you, leave it behind. Do be aware there are certain risks involved. The drastic cutting of carbs can result in certain side effects. This does include dizziness, fatigue weakness, headache, constipation, and more. You also need to be careful of nutritional deficiencies or a certain level of insufficient fiber. This can cause health problems such as diarrhea, nausea, and constipation.

You can consider adapting your Atkins diet by taking on recommendations such as a small number of salt supplements and vitamins. However, it is good to remember that the Atkins diet is not appropriate for everyone. It is best to always consult with a doctor before starting a diet, especially if you struggle with insulin resistance, diabetes, or you take diuretics medication. Furthermore, if you suffer from kidney disease, you should most certainly not follow this diet.

This diet is also not made for women who are pregnant or breastfeeding.

Intermittent Fasting Explained

Intermittent fasting is a quickly growing diet trend. Like all diet fads, it has its levels of successes and failures. It all depends upon how you approach it.

Intermittent fasting is an approach that works on a time-restricted form of eating. This means the times you eat and the times you fast are limited. You generally fast for 16 hours a day and eat for eight hours or less. There are also methods such as 24 hours fasting or the 12-hour fasting method.

A lot of the research tends to come from animal studies, but some human data has shown quite promising results in regards to the potential of weight loss and improving some aspects with nutrition. This is especially beneficial when it comes to diseases such as diabetes.

A fascinating fact about fasting is that it has been around for a while. Intermittent fasting is simply the modernized term for a concept that has been around for ages. In order to appreciate the physiology of fasting it is good to understand how it was used and what was used in history. It is known that the early stages of fasting can cause rapid weight loss. Sometimes it can cause almost two pounds a day for the first week. However, it does slow down about half a pound by the third week. Fasting is characterized as a high rate of glucose neogenesis. It means that ketosis starts due to the mobilization and the oxidation of fatty acids. As soon as ketone levels rise, they will replace glucose as a primary source of energy for the central nervous system. This decreases the need for glucose and it does pay for the protein. There are many hormonal changes that take place when you are fasting. This includes your levels of insulin and a rise in glucogenic levels. Many studies have actually found that obese people always lose more weight while fasting than those who are lean lose.

People have been fasting for centuries for religious or dietary reasons. Many doctors in ancient times recommended it as an integral method of healing as well as prevention of diseases. Hippocrates, the father of western medicine, firmly believed fasting enabled the body to heal itself. Paracelsus, who was another great doctor in the western tradition, wrote about 500 years ago about the benefits of fasting. Women in particular also seemed to be more active in religious fasting. They survived for weeks without nourishment, which was regarded as a sign of chastity and holiness.

In the 19th century, therapeutic fasting was used to treat or prevent health problems. This was done under medical supervision. There were many advocates for fasting, and considering this is a practice they've been using for so many years, it is not too far off to conclude that the benefits are truly legit. In Germany, fasting is used for therapeutic reasons and is offered in various centers. Certain German hospitals now run fasting for weeks on end. They are funded by health insurance programs that help to manage obesity.

Intermittent Fasting Benefits and Drawbacks

Intermittent fasting supports weight loss. The main goal of people adopting intermittent fasting is because of this. When you are fasting intermittently, you are restricting caloric intake which inevitably results in weight loss. Weight loss in and of itself helps reduce risks such as chronic diseases like high blood pressure, diabetes, stroke, and heart diseases.

There is a lot of speculation that weight loss only happens with intermittent fasting because of your calories. Some would say the fact that intermittent fasting helps you drop weight quickly makes it the perfect diet. However, there is more to the story. Studies have actually shown that short-term fasting could increase your metabolism which leads to more weight loss. This means that intermittent fasting plays a bigger role than simply cutting your calories. There is some controversy to this idea however and more studies need to be done in order to confirm this.

Intermittent fasting could potentially help with insulin resistance. Lower blood sugar has frequently been found in people who have been participating in intermittent fasting. It is believed that one of the major causes of type 2 diabetes is due to insulin resistance. High levels of insulin do exist in the bloodstream of a body that is often supplied with glucose. Your insulin levels are low in between meals. Therefore, it makes sense if you extend your fasting times it could result in a decrease in insulin. Intermittent fasting gives your body a break from glucose spikes. This can help minimize the resistance that comes from insulin. There are still studies being performed, but many people have claimed to see a difference as well as improved results in intermittent fasting and their diabetes. Some go as far as no longer needing their medication.

However, as usual, it is best to consult with a professional before taking on this form of diet because they are aware of your personal factors and history that a book cannot identify.

Intermittent fasting could potentially help reduce your cholesterol. It has been shown that lipid profiles have been reduced in overall cholesterol in people who take on intermittent fasting. This can also lower your triglycerides and boost your HDL. Again, there's not enough evidence to definitively claim fasting can help your cholesterol. There has to be more research done for scientists to be completely sure.

Another benefit that has been popping up is the idea that intermittent fasting could support heart health. It basically means that the risk factors of heart diseases such as hypertension and heart rate variability are improved. This is an exciting concept, but the studies have mostly been done on rats and mice. However, the results are looking promising, so one should really take this into consideration when taking on intermittent fasting.

Intermittent fasting has also been shown to promote better health through the reduction of inflammation. Acute inflammation is actually a process of the immune system used to help fight off infections. However, if you do get chronic inflammation it can actually lead to serious consequences for your overall health. Research has actually shown that information is involved in certain developments of chronic conditions such as cancer, heart disease, and rheumatoid arthritis. Fasting is also shown to help decrease certain levels of inflammation.

Fasting does have an effect on one's growth hormone secretion as well as your metabolism, growth, weight loss, and muscle strength. Believe it or not, fasting could potentially help you grow muscle mass. The human growth hormone HGH is an important aspect of health and weight loss. Fasting naturally increases your HGH levels. Fasting can also delay certain elements of aging.

Another theory about fasting is that it could aid in cancer prevention and increase the effectiveness that chemotherapy has. Taking on an alternate day of fasting could hinder tumor formation. When this happens, you are effectively helping chemotherapy get rid of cancer. However, the studies are limited to animals. While it cannot be confirmed for humans, it is a promising finding.

On the other hand, there are concerns when it comes to intermittent fasting. Intermittent fasting can lead to potential weight gain. The reason being is that if you have binging behaviors, you could end up overindulging in your non-fasting periods. This can make you gain weight. This is because you feel starved, it does cause stronger cravings when you are actually eating. The best tip to come back from this is to break your fasting with lean protein. The biggest reason why you get hunger cravings is that your body is lacking in protein. So it is best to make a meal plan as well as break your fast appropriately.

Another issue that might come your way is feeling tired and moody. It is a common complaint for people to feel irritability when taking on intermittent fasting. A person can also have impaired cognitive function while they are working. This can especially apply to people who take on extended periods of time when fasting. Therefore, it is best to stick to short-term fasting that is sustainable. You should also consider not starting cold turkey immediately. Some start off with 12 hours of eating and 12 hours of fasting. Push it up an hour extra of fasting until your body gradually gets used to it. It is best to work on it gradually rather than to try and go out at full speed. You may end up crashing into a wall and failing.

You will almost certainly find yourself experiencing side effects such as dizziness, headaches, and nausea. Considering that long periods of fasting can lead to lower blood sugar levels, it makes sense. Your body is not used to fasting and goes into survival mode. However, if you make fasting a routine habit a lot of these symptoms should go away over time. Do keep in mind that the decrease in your blood sugar levels could be dangerous if you are someone with type 1 diabetes or someone who is on diabetic medications. Even as a type 2 diabetic it is best to consult with a professional. Or if you suffer from low blood sugar it is so then better not take on intermittent fasting.

Additionally, if you struggle with eating disorders of any kind do not do intermittent fasting. Any diet that supports restrictive eating or skipping meals can actually trigger an unhealthy relationship with food, even if it has positive weight loss effects. If you feel you may take intermittent fasting too far, simply not do it. Make sure you are getting the nutrients you need to feed your body throughout the day, whether it is by taking supplements or planning your meals in your eating window accordingly. It is best to make sure that during this time you are getting enough food.

Wrapping Up The Diets

So to wrap things up, each diet form has its own unique and special benefit. As you may have noticed, most of them share many similarities, therefore there is no harm in trying different diet methods to find the right one. Furthermore, it is best to take on something that is sustainable for your lifestyle. When it comes to different food choices, you need to make sure you are happy and comfortable. For someone who is an avid meat lover, it may be painful to become a vegan. And for someone who does love their grains, maybe a carb restrictive diet isn't the way to go. It all depends upon what you are willing to sacrifice and how far you are willing to go to lose weight. It also depends upon your budget and lifestyle. It is truly up to you to decide what you can manage and how you can stay healthy and follow a good diet. Do keep in mind each and every diet plan has its flaws and it is best to compensate for them in some or another way. Whether it is through supplements, proper meal planning, or tweaking it even a little bit. The diet plan you decide is up to you, but it is best to get started and to stay motivated.

Chapter 7: Choosing a Diet For Your Lifestyle

So what are the steps you want to take in finding your life? When it comes to matters of weight loss you will find no shortage of advice from websites, books, and magazines that all promise you results. There are so many conflicting options you might wonder what you should choose for yourself. Here are some of the top suggestions on choosing your meal plan for your lifestyle.

It is generally best to involve your doctor with your weight loss program. The doctor can review your medical issues as well as the medications that might affect the program you want. They can also give you necessary and safe guidance, as well as help you devise a healthy program. You can also discuss forms of exercise, especially if you have physical or medical challenges. It is best to tell your doctor your whole history of weight loss. Your doctor should be able to point you in the right direction and direct you to weight loss support groups. This is especially handy if you would like to get in contact with a registered dietitian.

You do need to consider your own personal needs. There's no singular diet or plan for everyone. You have to take into consideration your preferences, weight loss goals, and lifestyle to find a diet that is specifically tailored to your needs. Before you start a weight-loss program there are things you need to think about.

Firstly, you need to consider any diet you have already tried. You need to think about what you liked about them and what you disliked about them. You also need to consider whether or not you were actually able to follow them and whether they were actually working. How did you feel emotionally or physically when you were on the diet?

You also need to consider your preferences. Do you prefer to do a weight-loss program completely on your own or would you like to have the support of a group? If you do like to have group support, would you want it to be on the web or in-person meetings?

Take a look at your budget. Certain weight loss programs do have the requirements for you to purchase supplements or meals. You could also visit weight loss clinics or support groups which do have their costs. Will these costs fit within your budget?

It is crucial to take into consideration whether or not you have health conditions, allergies, or diseases like diabetes. Are there any cultural preferences and requirements that you may have in regards to food? These are all things you need to take into consideration before picking a diet plan. Otherwise, you may find yourself stuck halfway with some pretty major issues. It is better to be prepared and plan beforehand than to be caught in the middle of a diet plan and have trouble.

Furthermore, as tempting as it may be to buy into rapid and dramatic weight loss promises, it is better to adopt the slow and steady approach, considering it tends to beat fast weight loss in the long run. It is normally recommended to lose about one-half to two pounds a week.

There are certain situations where faster weight loss can be quite safe if it is done right. These are normally low-calorie diets that are done on medical supervision or a brief quick-start phase that may occur in a healthy eating plan.

A successful weight loss program requires a long-term commitment. It should be a healthier lifestyle which not only changes what you are eating but also behavior and exercise needs over time. Behavior modification is certainly vital to your weight loss goals, as it has the greatest impact when it comes to your weight loss.

Make sure your plan is flexible and suited to your lifestyle. You need to look at a flexible plan that includes a variety of foods or major food groups. Some of the plans mentioned up above aren't as flexible, so you really have to take that into consideration. If you are all up for strict and control, then pick a diet that has rules. However, if you are someone who struggles, it is best to keep to a flexible diet.

You also need to consider balance. Your plan should certainly require adequate nutrients and calories. If extra supplements are recommended, be sure to keep an eye out for any symptoms of deficiency. It is normally a good idea to go for a diet that does not always require supplements. Be sure to keep yourself up to date on research surrounding your chosen diet.

You also need to pick a diet that you like, because if you enjoy what you are eating you are more likely to follow the plan. If you don't like the food which is on the plan you're more likely to fail.

Include physical activity in your diet plan. Exercise can give you a weight-loss boost. It also offers multiple health benefits including an increase in muscle mass. When muscle mass increases your body automatically burns more calories. Factoring in exercise is quite an advantage you give to yourself.

There are certain questions you should ask yourself when you are evaluating weight loss plans. Before diving into any kind of plan you need to learn as much as you can about it. Just because it is popular doesn't mean it will work for you.

- What is mainly involved? Does it teach you how to create positive and healthy changes in your life in order to maintain weight loss?
- You need to consider what is behind the diet. Is there any science and research in order to back up this weight loss approach? If you do happen

to go to a weight loss clinic, will there be trained professionals with experience?

- What are the risks normally involved? Could the weight loss program be very potentially harmful to your health?
- Are all their recommendations actually safe for you considering if you have medical conditions or do take certain medications?
- What are the results from people who have practiced this weight loss before you were here? How much weight do you actually expect to lose?
- And does a program make claims that he can lose a lot of weight quickly or very specifically targeting anybody?
- Do the before and after photos look a little too good to be true? And can you manage to maintain your weight loss over time after following this diet plan?

The most successful weight loss programs are long-term where you can change your eating habits and physical activity on a helping level. This means you need to approach and embrace the diet form for a lifetime. It is not likely that you are able to maintain the way to last unless you make changes afterward as well. A weight loss program should not meet a simple way of just shedding the pounds and returning back when you are done. It is best to always remain vigilant about your weight. Combining a healthier level of activity with a good diet is the best way to improve your health in the long term and to keep your weight off. It is best to take your time and find the answers necessary in order to take progressive steps forward in planning and preparing for your diet and weight loss journey.

How to Overcome The Mental Battles of Dieting

One of your biggest initial concerns could be whether or not you have the mental strength to follow through on a diet choice. It is easy to get started on anything, but following through in the long run is where most people fail. When it comes to dieting it is not a sprint, but a marathon. Weight loss is a painful process at times. You have to fight off cravings as well as self-doubt. This is why many people do not reach their target weights. There are many mental barriers that come in the way and can cause you to fail if you are not careful. And here are some things you can do to help fight it off.

The weight loss industry itself has ballooned to 61 Million Dollars. Many people follow weight loss programs that just don't work or they lose focus and are bound to fail over time. People try over and over again with weight loss programs, only to falter and stumble along the way. And even if people who have followed weight loss programs successfully lose the weight they wanted they somehow gain it all back.

This is a summary of the majority of most people's lives. How can you make sure yours is the exception?

People tend to gain motivation at the first signs of spring. This is normally a signal that it is the bathing suit season and a lot of people have been getting comfortable during the winter. This is a sign that most of the weight loss actually starts in your head. Having the right attitude can help you on your journey.

Everyone has their own excuses as to why they cannot lose weight. Whether it is the busy office hours that prevent you from having the ability to cook or exercise etc. They can improve their diet and their lifestyle until something happens. This is normal pressure issues in the family or even something else. It could be a personal issue or a certain pattern it actually needs to change if you want to be successful.

One of the biggest roadblocks you may come across with your weight loss is actually wanting too much too quickly, very much like a quick fix or a get-rich-quick scheme out in the world today. Everyone knows that such schemes tend to be scams. So, the same can be said for weight loss. A person can actually blame instant gratification society, because of the fact that everything happens fast.

Most people who fail want immediate results. Even though it technically took them many years to gain the weight, they want to lose weight within a couple of weeks. Getting the best results always shows when you lose weight slowly. When people lose a whole lot of weight it is normally because of water or lean tissue. It's not because they are losing fat - the thing people legitimately want to lose.

When you happen to lose lean tissue, your metabolism does actually slow down. This makes it infinitely harder to lose weight. Here are strategies for you to follow in order to think like and act like a person that has a healthy weight.

Visualizing your future self, whether it is a couple of months down the road or a year, will help you manifest your weight goals. think about how good you will look as well as feel at a healthy weight.

It is best to have very realistic expectations. When you have a goal weight, you need to pick a number that is realistic and attainable. It is best to consider a healthy weight range rather than a specific number. Picking a certain range to reach after a specific period of time will be much more encouraging than the simple number, especially if you fall outside the weight range.

It is recommended that you set yourself small goals under the bigger goals. Making a list of smaller goals can help you to achieve your weight loss goal. These smaller goals can help to improve your lifestyle without creating too much chaos or having it completely take over your life. These are goals such as ordering a side salad instead of potato chips, drinking alcohol only on weekends, increasing the number of fruits and vegetables to eat every day, or adding a certain level of physical activity. Make little changes each and every day.

Next, it is best to consider getting support. Everyone needs support during a tough time. Studies have shown that people who connect to others do better than those who try to go at it alone. If you think about it, how easy it is to dance at a party for a long time, but exercising on your own even for five minutes seems unbearable? This is all because of the social aspect that comes alongside it. Nobody wants to be alone when facing something difficult.

Next, it is wise to consider creating a detailed action plan. It is best to plan your healthy meals and fitness each day on a weekly basis. If you are equipped with a good plan you are more likely to have results. You need to schedule your fitness as if it were an appointment. Packing in healthy snacks will help you avoid the temptation of purchasing junk food. You can make your health a priority by building certain steps into your life. Create healthy behaviors as well as plans.

You need to learn to reward yourself. Giving yourself a pat on the back by treating yourself to fun activities such as watching a good movie. However, these rewards must not contain food. It shoots you in the foot if you reward yourself with the exact food that will set you back.

Slowly but surely, try to identify everything that you are engaging in that leads to weight gain. Take little steps as well so that you do not feel overwhelmed. For example, if you are normally a couch potato in the evening, consider changing the snacks you eat to fruit. and you can even start considering doing exercises while you watch the television.

The final step is to keep track of your weight loss journey. Weigh in regularly, perhaps once a week, and keep journals about what you eat. It is best to jot down your emotions, your exercises, and your weight measurement. Studies have shown that if you keep track of this information, it is more likely to help you promote positive behaviors. You must keep yourself accountable. You are less likely to make irrational decisions and you're more likely to think things through, which is a positive step in the weight loss regime.

Finding Your Voice

Another drawback that occurs for a lot of people is the social stigmas that arise when it comes to dieting and weight loss. This is where people claim to 'help' with their stinging comments when in reality it only hinders the weight loss journey of the person. Multiple times on multiple occasions have people gone to the gym for the very reason to lose weight, only to fall under severe scrutiny and lose their nerve. Even admitting that you are on a diet could get some hurtful responses, and here are certain steps you can take to find your voice and overcome this battle against the negative peers in your life.

Firstly, you need to be aware of what is out there. There are so many toxic perceptions about eating which people truly need to address. There is an idea that, unlike multiple other characteristics, weight can actually be under the control of people. Therefore, allowing excess stigma and stereotyping when people actually don't fit into the beauty standards, nor eat in the way that is perceived as 'healthy'.

On the flip side, when a person eats clean it can negatively affect how people perceive you. This means that it isn't a win-win situation and you are confronted with the reality that the choices you make are for your benefit and not for others. When you decide to eat healthily, it is a personal choice you will be undertaking and you need to realize that. Having the people around you bully you for your personal choices makes it tough, especially if you are struggling. Caving into what others might suggest is the easiest option, but it is certainly not the best. In fact, it's no surprise that most of the time people 'cheat' on their diets because of the influence of others. Which is majorly ironic. Here are some suggestions you can use when dealing with certain of these negative perceptions.

Keep in mind there is a common stereotype that people who go on diets are actually terribly unhappy, especially when they are restricting foods to lose weight. Yet again, when a person decides to eat healthily, it is not all about weight loss and you may find yourself having more energy as well as better health than your peers because of your choices. It is good to remind yourself of this when dealing with these certain comments. It is not merely for your weight, but for your overall health. In fact, you can remind your peers that you are very happy with the diet you are eating because of the benefits, and to remind them to please respect your decision and not push you into eating something you really do not want to.

Remind yourself as well that no one is actually too young to start eating healthy. If a person only changes their eating habits when they have health issues, they can make certain things pointless. The reason why is that a lot of the healthy eating benefits exist; because they work to reduce the risk of health complications, not really remove them when they have arrived.

Furthermore, when people tell you that you are missing out, it is almost as bad as telling someone they are missing out because they are not smoking. In reality, people know that certain foods are bad for you, so you are not missing much of anything. You can gently and respectfully remind them of that or repeat it to yourself when people make this argument against you.

Keep in mind, if people or certain friend groups keep pressuring you to break or cheat on your diet despite your protests and explanations, then you really need to reconsider the amount of time you spend with them. You do not have to necessarily cut them out of your life entirely, but rather avoid having meals with them if you know this is what is going to happen. Save yourself from the temptation as well as the trouble that may arise.

Taking Down Bad Habits

To conquer your bad habits it is best to be able to identify them at first. There might be some habits in regards to dieting that you are not even aware of. Many of these habits are unhealthy and potentially even hazardous for your health. It is best to get rid of them as soon as possible and each and every person has bad habits.

Firstly, a common bad habit is skipping breakfast. Unless you are taking on intermittent fasting, skipping the first meal of the day can slow down your metabolism and reduce the amount of energy productivity and concentration levels you have. Even though it has no major harmful effect, it can cause overeating throughout the rest of the day. This can help you manage your weight, which inevitably will help you live longer and feel better.

Unless you are specifically taking on a 24-hour fast, do not avoid food during the whole day. Whether it is through time constraints or simply a lack of resources available, you will end up overindulging at night. This is a common problem for people with demanding careers who find themselves overly busy during the day and eating at night. This can slow down your metabolism and when you overeat at night it will result in weight gain. Especially if you go to bed right after you had your meal. Try eating five or six small regular meals that are two to three hours apart. Remember to stick to the diet plan. If possible, figure out ways to slip in the meal or snack throughout the day if you can.

You should also consider cutting out any late-night snacking that may occur. Whether it is from eating a too small and late dinner or simply eating out of boredom. It is best to give your body time to digest and burn off the energy right before going to bed. Helping yourself to a snack so late at night will not help your weight loss goal.

Do not procrastinate. Do not tell yourself that you will start eating healthy next week or next month or next year. Your healthy choices can start literally with the meal in front of you. Whether it be at lunchtime or even supper time. Do not give up an entire day's worth of healthy meals if you indulge in a little unhealthy breakfast. Each and every meal should be considered as a fresh opportunity to boost your health.

Another unhealthy habit is having cravings for sweets. This normally comes from having a low blood sugar level. It is quite easy to pick up a sugary snack and even more so to carry on overindulging in it. Fixing this mistake is quite easy by keeping healthy snacks nearby. These healthy snacks can even be sweet or salty.

A person needs to watch out for overeating chocolate, but they do not have to cut it out in its entirety either. According to Herndon (2021), dark chocolate can improve your health and reduce the risk of diabetes by improving certain sensitivities with your insulin. However, this does mean you need to limit your chocolate intake as well as switch from white or milk to dark chocolate.

Additionally, you need to limit the number of times you go out to eat. Fast foods and restaurants have a reputation for having food high in sodium, as well as lacking in minerals and vitamins. The portions are certainly oversize and normally accompanied by sugary drinks. It is ironic enough that the drinks are even worse than the food in an oversized meal. It is practically scooping sugar in a bowl and eating it, and could potentially be one of the biggest bad habits most people have. It is best to eat something small before you go out as well as keeping a careful eye on the drink you order. You can even opt for healthier options that are on the menu such as vegetarian dishes and vegetable-based sauces instead of creamy options. Do not pick the supersize despite the cheap price, and choose fruit treats for dessert.

You also need to consider portions. It might be easy and cheap to purchase things in bulk, but this can cause you to overeat. You need to seriously consider reducing bulk purchases as well as ordering regular or small sizes in fast food restaurants. Even if it works out more expensive it has a more positive effect on your weight loss. When you are making food at home, choose smaller plates as well.

Oftentimes bad habits occur when you want to entertain guests. You end up making foods and dishes that are spectacularly unhealthy in order to keep them happy. Consider providing people with healthy meals and snacks such as lean meats and even vegetable side dishes. Be sure to offer low-calorie drinks or water. This will not only prevent you from being pressured into eating unhealthily, but you will also be benefiting others with your choices.

Another notoriously bad habit people have is a huge intake of salt. Many people are so automatic when they throw salt in their food without even really tasting it first. This can have an increased rate of hypertension as well as strokes. Remember to keep reading labels and make sure to monitor anything that has sodium in it. A better way to spice up your food is by using olive oil, lemon juice, peppers, and herbs. Even things such as cinnamon or curry can work to season your food.

Another notorious bad habit is someone who hops onto the latest diet fad. Not only can this help to slow down your metabolism, but it is normally unsustainable and impractical for your life.

A bad habit is exercising on an empty stomach. If you do not give your body fuel it means the body may break down your muscle to use for energy, rather than the fat you originally hoped for. A person needs glucose as energy in order to exercise according to the desired intensity. It is best to have a low GI (known as low Glycomic) meal two hours before an intense workout.

A bad habit that reverses a lot of your work is rewarding yourself with junk food after a workout. It is easy to grab a drink or two to reward yourself with junk food after having quite a massive exercise session. However, you need to focus on your carbs, protein, and electrolytes in order to recover efficiently. Otherwise, you might end up with the same issue as if you were exercising on an empty stomach. Your body additionally needs protein after a workout. This is only to help with the recovery after likely causing certain micro-tears in your muscles.

You also need to be extremely aware of emotional intent. Most people have a habit of eating for comfort. Having little habits such as this can be very dangerous for one's health. You really have to ask yourself whether you are hungry or stressed. Even boredom can cause a lot of stress eating or binge eating which inevitably results in weight gain.

Another massive mistake people make is going shopping on an empty stomach. When people are hungry you will find yourself desiring anything that you can see, even if it is not good for you. Consider eating an apple or full lunch before going to the shops. Be sure to write a proper shopping list that is in line with your diet plan as well.

You might opt for fruit juices as a healthy alternative to fizzy drinks. The problem with this is that they are loaded with sugar. In reality, even drinking something as innocent as orange juice up to 8.5 ounces can equate to about 60 grams of carbohydrates. This is nearly four slices of bread that are all just squeezed into your drink, which you may decide to drink in excess because it is meant to be a 'healthy drink. This is why your drinks can be one of the leading causes of weight gain. Sure, it can provide you with a lot of vitamins and minerals. However, fruit juices do not provide you with the fiber nor the feeling of satiation that a fresh fruit could get done. Focus on getting fresh fruit and water. If you absolutely want to have fruit juice, consider diluting it with water or a zero-calorie drink.

Another commonly bad habit is frying food. That is certainly the most energy-dense of all the macronutrients out there. Although it's not a bad thing to consume a healthy amount of fat, you do consume a lot of trans fat when you fry your food. Grill, boil, bake or even steam your food. It is certainly a lot healthier.

Lastly, another surprisingly bad weight loss habit is sleeping with the light on. Studies have actually found that having extreme light exposure at night can lead to weight gain. Also, be sure to get eight hours of sleep a night and keep it as dark as possible.

Another more common bad habit that most people are guilty of is snacking around the clock. Generally, snacking occurs with high-calorie foods that are normally full of infected carbohydrates. This is not just a problem for adults but for kids as well. Kids are also frequently snacking on unhealthy foods such as chips, candy, soda, and more. The best way to fix it is to keep snacks that are healthy within their reach. Hideaway unhealthy snacks or don't even buy them. You will be doing yourself a massive favor in the long run.

Do not wolf your food down. Even if it is merely a snack or meal. It basically means you are running ahead of your brain. Your brain does not really signal that you are full until about 20 to 15 minutes once you have started eating. So if you only eat within 5 to 10 minutes you could certainly end up eating a lot more than you actually need to. A lot of people who are overweight struggle with this problem. It is best to slow down eating. This is by physically forcing yourself to place your fork down as well as taking smaller bites and chewing slower. Drink water throughout your meal which can help you to slow down and feel fuller.

Adding New Habits

Now having learned to shed off bad habits, it is time to learn some good habits. It is like shedding a bad coat and putting on a brand new one. You need to start learning to embrace habits that a lot of people have taken on to succeed. Reaching your goals does require getting brand new attitudes, behaviors, and certainly a different mindset in order to enter the next level of health. If you want to get something new you always have to do something different. Do not expect to stay the same and have different results. People who are healthy reach their goal weight by managing these thoughts, habits, and attitudes. So what are some of these habits? Here are some things you need to certainly consider for your weight loss journey.

Firstly, people with healthy weights do not condemn themselves whenever they are actually enjoying what they eat. A toxic kind of thinking can lead to a toxic kind of behavior. Someone who enjoys what they eat and does not hate themselves for it is far better off than someone who eats and has a lot of conflicts internally.

It is best not to have any junk food or unhealthy snacks around. However, if it happens that not everyone adopts your form of eating, just ask them to keep those snacks out of sight. It best applies the concept: out of sight out of mind. This allows others to eat what they want. If you do want the occasional snack, consider taking a certain amount out of the bag and putting it away. Do not order oversized burgers, drinks, or fries, but rather go for the regulars or even small portions. People who have a healthy weight eat until they are full. This is certainly vastly different from eating until your plate is empty.

Sugary drinks are most certainly not a part of a daily diet when it comes to eating healthy. Healthy people stop eating before they actually have to unbutton their pants to finish their meal.

A common and good habit to take on is finding a way to comfort yourself that does not involve eating, whether it is through yoga, meditating, watching a movie, or even taking a nap.

When eating a meal, rather focus on taking your time and enjoying it. Allow yourself to have that lunch break, and certainly don't add any work or distractions. The slower you eat the better, rather than wolfing down the meals. It will allow you to feel full faster.

And a good habit to undertake to become a healthy weight is to cook instead of taking on the ease and convenience of fast foods.

Fast foods are additionally not the major sources of their meals. You should rather consider fast food as a treat instead of a regular meal from day to day. You also need to drink a lot of water. It is better to have water than any other kind of beverage.

A good habit for someone with a healthy weight is a person who actually eats with control. Learning to eat without overindulging or starving yourself is the best habit you can take on. You should also work on finishing your meal before even considering the next one coming later. For example, thinking about lunch while having breakfast, then considering dinner while having lunch are not good habits. Rather enjoy your meal set in front of you, and with a meal plan, you would not necessarily have to keep your mind occupied on what to eat next.

A good healthy habit would also be to stop eating at 8 p.m. Not because this is healthy but because it prevents you from late-night snacking. If you do find yourself not having eaten for a while then it is best to give you nutritious food. Deliberately deciding to make a little bit of effort even if it is late in the evening can certainly get you quite far.

Another amazing habit you should undertake is picking a regular bedtime and sticking to it. Whether you want to go to bed at 8:30 or even 12:30, it is certain that if you want to reduce your weight you need to go to bed at more or less the same time each and every day. People who go to bed on a consistent basis are more likely to have healthy body weight. This is because their sleep schedules are better structured.

Focus on the quality and not the quantity of your food. Counting a person's calories is a lot of work. And even so, some people still manage to gain weight. It is best to change your perspective and focus on the quality of your food, not necessarily the quantity. A normal body can process a whole lot more unprocessed foods without gaining weight in comparison to those who eat smaller portions of processed food.

It is best to be realistic with yourself, and undertake one or two habits at a time. This can help you to incorporate them all eventually without feeling too stressed or overwhelmed. Good habits certainly boost your health and are certainly going to boost your weight loss journey in and of itself.

Preventing Self-Sabotage

Removing bad habits and adding good habits may not quite cut it when it comes to your weight-loss journey. This is because it is not all about cheating on your diet. You want to avoid self-sabotaging your success and learn to work with yourself not against. This may be a funny idea considering that you want to lose weight, yet you may be the very person sabotaging your own efforts. How is this possible? This is because you are your own worst critic and you need to learn to convert any and all negative energy towards yourself into positive reinforcement. Here are some things you need to take on when focusing on your weight loss journey.

Firstly, making promises to yourself is nothing but small talk in your mind in reality. Making statements of visiting the gym every day or losing a certain amount of weight might not be enough. Making smaller steps for your goals will actually allow you to move forward at a slower but certainly steadier pace, and you are far more likely to stick to the plan than give up on discouragement.

Slow forms of this can be like adding another day of exercise on a weekly basis, then keeping it up for a month, or going to bed five minutes earlier each and every day until you reach those eight hours.

Face your fears. Fears normally cause procrastination for getting to the gym or finally starting up on that health plan. Start off by asking yourself, why are you afraid to go on that diet? But do not answer it by being weak or failing. You may be concerned with social stigma and bullying. The moment you however start to notice the fear is the moment you actually have the ability to start overcoming it.

Next, it is best to start breaking off from old patterns. This is one of the listed bad habits: eating as a reward for emotion. This is time to dig a little deeper and write down exactly what is going on when you are slammed with a food craving. Be aware of the thoughts that naturally pop up in your mind, if it is negative, write it down and analyze it objectively. But stay away from that fridge.

Once you start writing down your feelings and emotions, you find your need to emotionally dissipate which will make you feel overall better in the long run.

Furthermore, you should never be embarrassed over the fact that you are on a diet. Many times people feel ashamed for having made changes in their food choices, hiding them, and even cheating on their diets for the sake of avoiding confessing that they are trying to lose weight and live a healthier life. If you are feeling this way you are not alone, and many people have even tackled these diets on their own because of the feeling of 'shame'.

Yet the word diet should not be seen as a dirty word. No one should have to feel ashamed for making certain changes in their life in regards to food. Especially not if they have many goals in mind in regards to their dict. Most pcoplc do go on a diet at some point in their life so why should it be so heavily stigmatized?

So never feel ashamed about going on a diet. Find yourself a good support system, whether online or trusted friends and family. If anyone mocks you for your choices it is truly on them, and it is best to avoid and ignore their negative opinions. Rather focus on your health, your mentality, and your overall journey of health when it comes to your diet.

How To Draw Up A Meal Plan

So now you understand both bad habits and good habits. This will help you overcome the mental barriers that will head your way when facing a healthy lifestyle change. The next step would be to draw up a healthy meal plan. This will obviously be adapted to a diet of your choice. It might seem like an overwhelming practice, but it isn't if you plan ahead of time. This is when all the recipes have been decided upon as well as having been shopping for. Having to decide on gathering all the information about what you are going to eat for breakfast, lunch, and dinner can be quite difficult.

Here are some of the simplest steps you can take when selecting recipes and shopping for your ingredients, as well as preparing meals. These steps can actually seem to be quite obvious. Because as a matter of fact, they are. There is a critical and important strategy based on each and every one of them. This strategy can certainly turn your meal planning around as well as a heap in your success in weight loss.

Firstly, what exactly is meal planning? Meal planning is essentially asking the question of what you're going to eat for the whole week. Normally people plan meals day-to-day. A meal plan in essence has the same importance as a budget because it prepares you for where your money and your meals are going to go. It helps to prevent you from faltering and overeating and is the winning strategy when undertaking a diet.

Keep in mind meal planning can help change your life and there are multiple benefits that come your way. You need to allow yourself a lot of leeway to experiment and find exactly what works for you. Do keep in mind that meal planning is not kept in a big binder as your monthly records of meals. You can write it simply in a planner or on a simple piece of paper that you stick on the fridge, or you can simply create a document on your computer. It does not need to be a binder and it should be visible to you. Secondly, you do not have to plan home-cooked meals each and every day. You can plan a take-out once a week as a treat, so long as it is healthy. If you can, plan meals for everyone living in the house. There are different strategies that you might have to undertake with this, but if you are unable to it is not the end of the world. If you are flying solo, the meal planning tips will certainly help you out. It might also be easier, in the long run, considering there is no longer peer pressure to eat what others are eating around you. New planning if done right can save you money. Initially, it could end up being a little expensive, especially when you are stocking up on healthy foods for the first time. You will certainly see that this practice actually saves you money in the long run.

Meal planning is also not a lot of work. Starting out your meal plan can take a certain amount of concentrated time upfront. However, the moment you get things rolling is the moment it starts to get quicker. The first time you do anything seems to be slower. You just need to work out the details and experiment with what you like until you find a meal plan that suits you the best. This can take a couple of weeks to a couple of months, it all depends on how much you would like to experiment.

So when starting out a meal plan you do need to do a little bit of soul searching. The easiest way to answer all these questions is to consider exactly why you are interested in planning your meals. That will establish your initial goals as well as motivating you to move forward. Here are a few questions you can ask yourself.

Are you looking to add variety to your meals? Are you looking to save money? Are you looking to eat better and healthier as well as lose weight?

You do want to prevent wasting food in the long run. On the bright side, if you are within a family, creating a meal plan will also allow you to answer your partner or children the question of what is for dinner?

New planning can entail a lot, but do keep in mind it is best to start meal planning slowly just like adding new habits and removing old habits. Take it one step at a time and you will be surprised with how far you get. Start your meal plan at the end of your work week so you can shop on and prepare food on your days off.

Firstly you do need to choose the recipes you have very carefully. Choosing the recipes does put the philosophy and plan into action. It is potentially the most critical step in this whole process. You must not pick just a bunch of random recipes and hope for the best. You need to think about your meal plan a few days before you go shopping. Picking up the ingredients for recipes and your diet plan will have a major effect on your shopping list and the preparation of your meals. Here are a few steps on what to do to decide on your recipes.

You firstly need to decide how many meals to plan for and what exactly you actually need to do. You need to take a look at your calendar for the upcoming week as well as decide upon the number of nights you want to cook dinner. The five nights out of seven is the best choice, but some people find that even three nights is exactly what they need and can manage. Even if you cook only for three nights, you can certainly eat leftovers for two. You also need to consider the amount of time you have to cook. With the amount of time you have, you can decide upon your recipes as well.

Here are four rules you can follow to make sure you pick the right recipe for yourself. Choose meals that will leave you with leftovers. This is a practical reality where you save yourself time and effort to consistently have to cook a new meal from scratch.

Another rule is to cook and use recipes you know and add a new recipe from time to time. This can help you master a list of recipes over a certain period in a realistic and reasonable manner. It is also fun to add a variety, but not so much that you get overwhelmed. It is also based on choosing recipes based on common ingredients. This can save your wallet as well as your budget. Take into account what you already have in your pantry and kitchen. Unless you have the budget to start from scratch, then it is best to take all these things into consideration. Finally, you need to cook the things you actually want to eat. If you cook things you hate you will not find yourself motivated to cook at all. Try a new recipe, and if you don't like it after the first try, consider finding a new one. The internet and cookbooks have so many recipes available for you to try out. Therefore, you're not forced to try out one singular recipe and stick to it. If you don't like it, leave it.

The next step is to take on a two-step process to build an effective and accurate grocery list. This will let you have everything you need for your recipes. First, you need to make a master ingredient list. This is not your shopping list, but it will lead to one. This is more of an inventory of what is in your kitchen and what exactly you need. You will start off by listing all the recipe ingredients. Make sure you do not miss anything. Then go into the kitchen and scratch out anything that you already have. This will create a very accurate list that you can convert into your grocery list. The next step is to make a grocery list. This way you know everything that you need and if there are any extras that you want to add you can add them on there. It is also great to double-check on the ingredients as well as drawing up a better-organized list. You can use an app or a piece of paper. It is ideal if you organize your shopping list by the ingredients that go in the different departments in each grocery store. If you want to take it a step further, you need to put the sections in the order which you would actually like to hit in the store. This means you actually need to know the store you want to visit as well as its layout. This actually takes a decent bit of time, so this is a skill that will be developing as well as your meal plan.

After you have picked the recipes, made the grocery list, and shopped for your meals it is time to turn your plan into action. This is when you start cooking dinners, lunches, and breakfasts.

There is one more step you can take to help yourself out. This is known as preparation: meant to combat any form of cooking fatigue you could experience throughout the week. It is recommended to set aside at least one hour before the start of your week for bulk cooking. Whatever you do entirely depends upon the recipes you may have. But doing all the shopping, washing as well as preparing the meat can always be a massive help as when you actually need to do the cooking during the working days. You can even consider cooking several meals in bulk and saving it in the freezer.

Now after you have completed your first meal plan, you will realize that meal planning is not so difficult after all. You will have to be a bit more flexible as well as to adapt to disasters that may occur in the beginning. Everyone makes mistakes so don't think it won't happen to you. Your first plan won't be perfect, but be gracious with yourself. This is a learning curve a lot of people have gone through. Now you are adopting a healthier habit than most people are not undertaking. This is one where you are deciding to change your life and your weight. So be proud, especially if you have come this far to make such beautiful changes.

Conclusion

Now you have reached the end of the line. This is where you have found the knowledge necessary to take action and make the decisions to change your life. Keep in mind all the obstacles that you may have to overcome, both physical and mental. Remember, every diet has benefits and drawbacks.

Your next moves are entirely up to you. Which diet suits your liking and what would you like to adapt it with? You know your lifestyle and you know your career. You know when you want to get up in the morning as well as when you want to go to bed. Each person has a very different life in this world. To expect the same results for everyone is not only unfair but cruel. So don't be cruel to yourself and don't be unfair either. If everyone was the same, the world would be a perfectly boring place. This is an odd thing to say in the book about weight loss yet, it is so important to be reminded of this. If a person isn't unique and if a person doesn't have their own sets of struggles, how do they grow? Weight loss is a form of growth. It is ironic to think about how certain people can struggle to pick up weight when you just can't wait to lose it. Yet, the truth remains the same. We all have our struggles. It is best to embrace it as it is and keep moving forward. Your life will be so much more motivating when you realize that you have grown extensively as well as changed for the better.

The truth shines very clearly and will not leave. Remind yourself to take it slowly, one step at a time. Even if you do not want to adopt a singular diet form, maybe consider taking some of the strategies surrounding them for your overall benefit. Many of the tricks and tips can truly accumulate your weight loss success journey, and you may just be surprised at the outcome at the end of the day. Remember to keep yourself responsible, and to keep track of your process. Even ideas such as weighing yourself once a week or taking pictures once a month can work as a major motivating factor. The moment you see progress it can turn your struggling uphill to a more eased downhill. You will find the rewards to be addictive, even more so than sugar. This is a mountain you will have to overcome. However, once you reach the top it is quite simple from thereon. You will have gone through an incredibly rewarding journey. People who start helping lives and push through tend to remain in the long haul. But it is that mountain that they need to cross. So now you're left with one single question. Will you take on this mountain and the climb?

References

Benefits of a balanced diet. (2021). *Who.int*. https://doi.org/https://www.euro.who.int/en/health-topics/disease-prevention/nutrition/a-healthy-lifestyle/benefits-of-a-balanced-diet

Brazier, Y. (2020, April 24). *Dukan diet: Should I try it?* Medicalnewstoday.com; Medical News Today. https://www.medicalnewstoday.com/articles/219612#phases

Campos, M. (2017, July 27). *Ketogenic diet: Is the ultimate low-carb diet good for you? - Harvard Health*. Harvard Health; Harvard Health. https://www.health.harvard.edu/blog/ketogenic-diet-is-the-ultimate-low-carb-diet-good-for-you-2017072712089

Can a low-carb diet help you lose weight? (2020). Mayo Clinic; https://www.mayoclinic.org/healthy-lifestyle/weight-loss/in-depth/low-carb-diet/art-20045831#:~:text=Definition,of%20carbohydrates%20you%20can%20eat.

Crichton-Stuart, C. (2020a, November 26). *What are the benefits of eating healthy?* Medicalnewstoday.com; Medical News Today. https://www.medicalnewstoday.com/articles/322268#heart-health

Crichton-Stuart, C. (2020b, November 26). *What are the benefits of eating healthy?* Medicalnewstoday.com; Medical News Today. https://www.medicalnewstoday.com/articles/322268#the-next-generation

Dashti, H. M., Mathew, T. C., Hussein, T., Asfar, S. K., Behbahani, A., Khoursheed, M. A., Al-Sayer, H. M., Bo-Abbas, Y. Y., & Al-Zaid, N. S. (2004). Long-term effects of a ketogenic diet in obese patients. *Experimental and Clinical Cardiology*, *9*(3), 200–205.

https://www.ncbi.nlm.nih.gov/pmc/articles/PMC2716748/

debbie. (2021). *Phases for Low Carb Diet Plan Explained - Dukan Diet 4 Phases*. Weight Loss Diet Plan & Coaching - Dukan Diet. https://www.dukandiet.com/low-carb-diet/4-phases

Diet myths and facts: MedlinePlus Medical Encyclopedia. (2013). Medlineplus.gov. https://medlineplus.gov/ency/patientinstructions/000895.htm

Gotter, A. (2020, January 7). *Why is the keto diet good for you?* Medicalnewstoday.com; Medical News Today. https://www.medicalnewstoday.com/articles/319196#takeaway

Gunnars, K. (2018, November 20). *10 Health Benefits of Low-Carb and Ketogenic Diets*. Healthline; Healthline Media. https://www.healthline.com/nutrition/10-

benefits-of-low-carb-ketogenic-diets#TOC_TITLE_HDR_2

http://www.facebook.com/therecipecritic. (2016, May 29). *Creamy Tuscan Garlic Chicken | The Recipe Critic*. The Recipe Critic. https://therecipecritic.com/creamy-tuscan-garlic-chicken/

https://www.facebook.com/budgetbytes1. (2019, December 15). *Meal Planning 101 - How to Make a Custom Meal Plan - Budget Bytes*. Budget Bytes. https://www.budgetbytes.com/meal-planning-101-how-to-make-a-meal-plan-that-works-for-you/

Kiah Connolly, MD. (2020, November 21). *Intermittent Fasting Pros and Cons: What the Science Says*. Trifectanutrition.com; Trifecta Nutrition. https://www.trifectanutrition.com/blog/intermittent-fasting-pros-and-cons-should-you-try-it

Kubala, J. (2018, April 24). *8 Symptoms of Caffeine Withdrawal*. Healthline; Healthline Media.

https://www.healthline.com/nutrition/caffeine-withdrawal-symptoms#TOC_TITLE_HDR_8

McDowell, E. (2018, May 9). *Ketogenic Baked Eggs and Zoodles with Avocado*. PureWow; PureWow. https://www.purewow.com/recipes/ketogenic-baked-eggs-and-zoodles-with-avocado

Mercey Livingston. (2020, June 26). *Everything you need to know about a vegan diet, explained*. CNET; CNET. https://www.cnet.com/health/nutrition/what-is-a-vegan-diet-how-to-get-started/

News-Medical. (2017, July 18). *Paleo Diet: Pros and Cons*. News-Medical.net. https://www.news-medical.net/health/Paleo-Diet-Pros-and-Cons.aspx

Paleo diet: Eat like a cave man and lose weight? (2020). Mayo Clinic; https://www.mayoclinic.org/healthy-lifestyle/nutrition-and-healthy-eating/in-depth/paleo-diet/art-20111182#:~:text=A%20paleo%20diet%20typically%

20includes,dairy%20products%2C%20legumes%20and%20grains.

Petre, A. (2016, November). *The Vegan Diet — A Complete Guide for Beginners*. Healthline; Healthline Media. https://www.healthline.com/nutrition/vegan-diet-guide#TOC_TITLE_HDR_4

Santos-Longhurst, A. (2020, July 28). *What Is a Sugar Detox? Effects and How to Avoid Sugar*. Healthline; Healthline Media. https://www.healthline.com/health/sugar-detox-symptoms#managing-side-effects

Schaefer, A. (2020a, April 30). *Experts Agree: Sugar Might Be as Addictive as Cocaine*. Healthline; Healthline Media. https://www.healthline.com/health/food-nutrition/experts-is-sugar-addictive-drug#What-is-an-addiction?

Schaefer, A. (2020b, April 30). *Experts Agree: Sugar Might Be as Addictive as Cocaine*. Healthline;

Healthline Media. https://www.healthline.com/health/food-nutrition/experts-is-sugar-addictive-drug#What-is-an-addiction?

Schaefer, A. (2020c, April 30). *Experts Agree: Sugar Might Be as Addictive as Cocaine*. Healthline; Healthline Media. https://www.healthline.com/health/food-nutrition/experts-is-sugar-addictive-drug#What-is-an-addiction?

Schaefer, A. (2020d, April 30). *Experts Agree: Sugar Might Be as Addictive as Cocaine*. Healthline; Healthline Media. https://www.healthline.com/health/food-nutrition/experts-is-sugar-addictive-drug#What-is-an-addiction?

The Top 8 Psychological Barriers to Weight Loss. (2015, July 16). VeraVia Fitness.

https://veraviafit.com/2015/07/16/the-top-8-psychological-barriers-to-weight-loss/

Veganism is “single biggest way” to reduce our environmental impact on planet, study finds. (2020, September 24). *The Independent*. https://www.independent.co.uk/life-style/health-and-families/veganism-environmental-impact-planet-reduced-plant-based-diet-humans-study-a8378631.html

Ware, T. S. (2018, September 10). *23 Habits That Keep Skinny People Skinny — Exercise Is Not On This List*. Medium; Medium. https://medium.com/@tonyasware/23-habits-that-keep-skinny-people-skinny-exercise-is-not-on-this-list-42f61182d86a

Watson, S. (2013, December 11). *The Blood Type Diet*. WebMD; WebMD. https://www.webmd.com/diet/a-z/blood-type-diet

Weight loss: Choosing a diet that's right for you. (2020). Mayo Clinic; https://www.mayoclinic.org/healthy-lifestyle/weight-loss/in-depth/weight-loss/art-20048466

Wong, C. (2014, August 20). *What Is the Blood Type Diet?* Verywell Fit; Verywell Fit. https://www.verywellfit.com/the-blood-type-diet-89893

Zelman, K. M. (2007, April 19). *8 Ways to Think Thin.* WebMD; WebMD. https://www.webmd.com/diet/obesity/features/8-ways-to-think-thin#3

www.ingramcontent.com/pod-product-compliance
Ingram Content Group UK Ltd.
Pitfield, Milton Keynes, MK11 3LW, UK
UKHW022001270726
14060UKWH00003B/620